# THE 1% IMPACT

THE 1% IMPACT

# THE 1% IMPACT

*How to Transform Your Life
in 15 Minutes a Day*

ERIK WESTRUM

The 1% Impact | Erik Westrum | © Copyright 2024

All rights reserved. No part of this publication may be reproduced, distributed, or transmitted in any form or by any means, including photocopying, recording, or other electronic or mechanical methods, without the prior written permission of the publisher, except in the case of brief quotations embodied in critical reviews and certain other noncommercial uses permitted by copyright law.

Although the author and publisher have made every effort to ensure that the information in this book was correct at press time, the author and publisher do not assume and hereby disclaim any liability to any party for any loss, damage, or disruption caused by errors or omissions, whether such errors or omissions result from negligence, accident, or any other cause.

Adherence to all applicable laws and regulations, including international, federal, state, and local, governing professional licensing, business practices, advertising, and all other aspects of doing business in the US, Canada, or any other jurisdiction, is the sole responsibility of the reader and consumer.

Neither the author nor the publisher assumes any responsibility or liability whatsoever on behalf of the consumer or reader of this material. Any perceived slight of any individual or organization is purely unintentional.

The resources in this book are provided for informational purposes only and should not be used to replace the specialized training and professional judgment of a health care or mental health care professional.

Neither the author nor the publisher can be held responsible for the use of the information provided within this book. Please always consult a trained professional before making any decision regarding treatment of yourself or others.

Ebook: 979-8-89694-203-0
Paperback: 979-8-89694-204-7
Hardcover: 979-8-89694-205-4

# Get Your Free Gift

To get the best experience with this book, I've found that readers who download and use the accompanying guide, *How to Guarantee Results in 30 Days Using the 1% Impact*, can implement change faster and take the next steps needed to level up their lives. The 1% impact strategy focuses on consistent, small improvements that compound over time, achieving guaranteed results in 30 days. Making daily progress—improving by just 1% every day—can lead to significant change by the end of the 30 days.

I'm excited to give you this road map to lead you on your personal journey and get you started in becoming the new you. After all, I know you have the desire to improve, and whatever is holding you back, I guarantee I'll help you overcome what's in your way—1% at a time. Now let's go!

Visit www.erikwestrumbook.com to get your free gift today, or scan the QR code to access it right now.

# Dedication

My beloved family and cherished friends: your steadfast support and love have been my greatest inspiration. Thank you for believing in me and for every moment we've shared. This journey wouldn't be the same without you.

My wife, Kelly, for her unwavering ability to level up 1% at a time in raising our four wonderful kids.

My kids, Luke, Ethan, Isabella, and Evelina, for continuing to live a life following Jesus and believing in yourself in everything you do. Keep putting in the extra 1% each day, and your dreams will become your reality.

My parents, for laying the foundation and paving the way to allow me to grow into who I am today; for the freedom to be me and find my path.

My teammates, coaches, and business colleagues, for the lessons learned over the past years through blood, sweat, and tears, along with the wins, losses, and championships that have taught me a lot about life.

Every interaction I have continues to bless me in more ways than I could ever imagine. I have truly found my passion and purpose in life. Thank you to those who have crossed my path and to those I will someday meet in the journey of life.

# Foreword

Success doesn't just happen, it's built. It's the result of intentionality, consistent effort, and a mindset that refuses to settle for average. That's why *The 1% Impact* resonates so deeply with me. In this book, Erik Westrum has captured a powerful truth: real greatness isn't achieved in grand, fleeting moments, but in small, purposeful actions we take every single day.

In sports, we talk about being ELITE. That word gets thrown around so easily, but it's more than a label—it's a way of life. Being ELITE is about embracing the grind, attacking life with a Nekton mentality, and finding joy and peace in the journey. Knowing everything you are doing is truly the best you can do. It's about holding yourself to the highest standard in every area of your life, even when no one else is watching. It's not just about winning the game; it's about winning the day, the week, the month and even the minute.

Erik's message of leveling up and playing up by committing just 15 minutes a day is not just practical, it's transformational. He challenges you to focus on what matters, take ownership of your time, and make the choice to improve by 1% daily. This approach aligns perfectly with what I teach my players. Row The Boat! Rowing isn't about perfection or instant results; it's about consistent effort, commitment, and belief in the process.

Life doesn't hand out guarantees, and everyone is looking for an edge to get ahead. The only things we control are how we show up, our attitude, our effort, and our willingness to grow. HOW we think and HOW we act allow us to get ahead in life. Erik understands this, and he lays out a roadmap for anyone ready to take their life, their leadership, and their potential to the next level.

This book is a true hat trick for positive change in your life. Erik gives us a reminder that success isn't about massive leaps, but about steady progress filled with changing your best 1% daily. It's about the discipline to do the little things well and the courage to keep going when the going gets tough. If you commit to the principles Erik shares here, you'll discover the incredible power of incremental growth—not just in achieving your goals, but in transforming who you are along the way.

So, grab an oar, set your vision and course, and row toward the person you were meant to become. *The 1% Impact* is your guide to building a life of purpose, excellence and—yes—an ELITE mindset!

P. J. Fleck
Head Football Coach, University of Minnesota
*Wall Street Journal* Best-Selling Author of *Row the Boat*

# CONTENTS

| | |
|---|---|
| **FOREWORD** | IX |
| **INTRODUCTION** | 1 |
| **THE MAGIC OF 1%** | 7 |
| Things to Know | 9 |
| Current Self vs. Future Self | 13 |
| If You Believe, You Will Achieve | 19 |
| Confidence vs. Humility | 25 |
| | |
| **WHO** | 33 |
| Reliability vs. Stability | 34 |
| Complacency vs. Consistency | 42 |
| Collaboration vs. Competition | 50 |
| | |
| **WHAT** | 61 |
| Resiliency vs. Perseverance | 62 |
| Focus vs. Concentration | 69 |
| Reality vs. Optimism | 75 |
| | |
| **WHERE** | 85 |
| Motivation vs. Discipline | 86 |
| Fixed vs. Growth Mindset | 93 |
| Time vs. Priority Management | 99 |

## WHEN — 107

Responsibility vs. Accountability — 108
Fear vs. Courage — 116
Follower vs. Leader — 123

## WHY — 135

Thankfulness vs. Gratitude — 136
Forgiveness vs. Grace — 142
Happiness vs. Joy — 150

## HOW — 159

Outcome vs. Process — 160
Strategy vs. Planning — 169
Goals vs. Vision — 177

## TAKE A STEP — 187

Two Options — 188
The Importance of Change — 193
Take Action — 195

## ACKNOWLEDGEMENTS — 201
## AUTHOR BIO — 203

# Introduction

As I stepped out on stage at one of the biggest financial conferences in downtown Minneapolis to speak about becoming elite and what it takes to be in the 1%, it dawned on me: I was part of the 1% of hockey players to play in the NHL. I had made it. I had committed myself to becoming one of the best in the world at a game I had loved for as long as I could remember. But now I wasn't on the ice doing what I knew best: skating, shooting, and competing with my teammates to win. Instead, I was on stage all alone, like a goldfish swimming around a fishbowl.

I froze.

I took one step forward and two steps back. I wondered if I could *really* do this at such a high level. Yes, I had given "one-off" keynote talks before, but nothing like this one. I began questioning myself. What knowledge and expertise did I have to share?

I looked in a nearby mirror located on the wall as I was about to step on stage and told myself, "Erik, snap out of it. Get it together."

That was the first time I truly understood what it was like to fall into the trap of imposter syndrome. I wondered to myself, *Why is this happening now? Why don't I believe in myself?*

After all, I had competed for the Minnesota State High School Championship as a young 16-year-old hockey player in front of 20,000 fans. I had been cool, calm, and collected.

In college my teammates and I sold out every game for four consecutive years as we grew into National Championship contenders from ages 18 to 21. I didn't have a worry in the world back then—I just focused on competing and being the best.

Stepping onto the ice for my first NHL hockey game in the brand-new arena in Glendale, Arizona, I didn't even flinch. Well, maybe a little. But after my first shift, I knew that I belonged at this level, competing with and against the best in the world: Steve Yzerman, Joe Sakic, Mike Modano, Jaromir Jagr, Peter Forsberg, Mats Sundin, Shane Doan, Brian Rolston, Chris Drury—the list goes on. This gave me confidence and created the opportunity to compete, not only against elite players in the NHL, but against the best players around the world.

I also had the honor of playing for Team USA at the highest level for the Men's National Team. I was the one chosen to take the winning shootout attempt to secure the bronze medal in front of tens of thousands of screaming fans. I knew I could do it, and I did—the kid from Apple Valley, Minnesota, scored the winning goal and delivered a bronze medal victory.

I was blessed, from an early age to the time I retired at the age of 33 with both individual and team accomplishments. Looking back, I realize I had confidence, discipline, and drive, pushing myself to be the best every day. At the time, I didn't fully understand I was following my own proven process. It wasn't until I faced the fateful transition to "life after hockey" that I realized how much I had invested in my career—and how little I knew about becoming elite in life.

Or did I? Yep, you guessed it: the light bulb went on, and that's how my first book, *Becoming Elite*, was born. I wrote my first book to help transform people's lives through my four proven pillars of performance.

I looked at the definition of elite and realized it could apply to anyone. After all, *elite* is defined as being "superior in terms of ability or qualities compared to the rest of the group or society." It is your desire to become a better version of yourself. It's not something that is simply given to you; it's something you have to earn. Sometimes people get stuck in a rut or don't feel worthy of becoming elite. The truth is, anyone has the potential to become elite, but in order to do so, you first need to take control of your life.

After realizing this, I wondered, *Why can't what helped me become part of the 1% in hockey be the same recipe to help me make it in life?* I'm here to tell you that it can, and it did.

I finally continued taking one step after the other toward the stage. I looked up at the big jumbotron and the huge screens scattered throughout the packed event center that read: *Erik Westrum–Becoming Elite–What it takes to transform your life using 4 proven pillars of performance*—and it clicked.

That's it.

Everything I'd been doing to prepare myself to be in the top 1% in hockey could easily translate to success in my new journey in life.

I needed to accept that I was in a different place, doing something completely different... but I also needed to understand that, deep down, it was all the same. If I continued to put in the work, show up every day, and hold onto my confidence, I would be able to keep climbing to new heights. I needed to stay in a growth mindset and not worry about failure. I just had to continue going above and beyond—1% at a time. That's when the results would come.

But I wondered, when would it happen? And how would I know when I had arrived?

That is the million-dollar question we all strive to answer, and guess what? The answers lie within the pages ahead! Your journey will be different from my journey, but in the end, if you level up your life 1% at a time, anything can happen!

Beyond these pages, you're going to learn how far 1% can really take you. It's the difference between being average and being elite. This is your choice, not mine. Some of you will say that you're all in, but soon realize you're only a pretender and not a true contender.

So are you willing to put a stake in the ground, draw a line in the sand, and make no excuses from this day forward to improve your life 1% at a time? If the answer is yes, then what are you waiting for? Let's go make a 1% impact in your life today!

# The Magic of 1%

Let's pull the rabbit out of the hat right away. No illusions here. Whenever I speak, I ask the audience what 1% of a day is in minutes. They always look around, think about it, guess, and then guess some more. Eventually someone will take out a phone, pull up the calculator app, and type in 24 hours x 60 minutes. Just so you know, that equals 1,440 minutes. Follow that up with 1,440 x 1%, and you get your answer: someone shouting out "14.4 minutes."

Yep, that's right. It's only 15 minutes per day. Why the math lesson? Wait around a bit and you'll see.

Once we establish the time frame, I'll ask someone what is the one physically active thing they want to accomplish in the next year, and 99% of people say the same thing. Someone usually yells, "I want to exercise more to get in better shape."

I proceed to ask, "Are you willing to commit 90-plus hours in the next year to exercise?"

Aghast, they usually look at me and shake their heads. "Ninety hours? I barely have 90 seconds to spare in a day."

I then follow up with what I call the "aha moment." Remember when I said we were pulling the rabbit out of the hat? This is when that happens, because I tell them, "How about just putting in 1%? That's 15 minutes per day put towards exercising this year."

The confidence returns. "Only 15 minutes? Of course I can do that this year."

That's right. Fifteen minutes per day for 365 days is just over 90 hours. And that is the magic of the 1% impact.

When you sit back and think about your day right now, do you think you could commit to adding 15 minutes to improve your life? Where could you add in that extra 1%? Maybe it's waking up 15 minutes earlier to read the Bible, exercise, or even go for a walk. Maybe it's blocking off 15 minutes in the middle of the day to meditate, work out, or write in your journal. Or maybe it's time you can locate before bed when you can take inventory of your day, get in a nighttime jog, or write 500 words towards your first book, which is exactly what I did. Over a 60-day time frame, writing only 15 minutes per day, I completed this book.

No matter when you fit it in or what you do with your 1% impact, I can guarantee it will change your life.

How?

Simple. When you are willing to move the needle and take one step forward to becoming a new you, that is when the magic happens.

## Things to Know

In the pages ahead, you'll be challenged to look at what is holding you back from making that 1% impact in your life. I've found the easiest way to dig deeper into your own life is to go one layer past the four proven pillars discussed in my first book. If you haven't read it yet, I recommend you grab a copy! But for those who haven't had the time to read *Becoming Elite* yet, here is a quick cheat sheet to help you understand the foundation behind Becoming Elite.

### Pillar One: Psychological Shift

The mind is the most powerful tool we possess, and that is why the first pillar of performance is the psychological shift in our lives. This is the shift from a fixed mindset to a growth mindset. It's the start of getting outside your comfort zone.

### Pillar Two: Physical Shift

As we transition from our mind to our body, it is important to understand the physical shift will look different from person to person. This is especially true when you consider the level of activity you've been accustomed to throughout your life. It will also be dictated by your enjoyment, or lack thereof, of certain activities. Now is the right time to start taking care of your current self! Your future self will thank you.

## Pillar Three: Spiritual Shift

The spiritual shift isn't about declaring a certain religion or belief. Instead, it's about taking a journey to find out who you are, what problems you face in your life, and how you can come to peace with today's world. The main purpose of the spiritual shift is oftentimes not finding the answer or solution, but learning how to start the continual process of asking questions. It is important to listen to your mind, body, and soul together as one.

## Pillar Four: Emotional Shift

When I was playing sports, I was often told to control my emotions. Don't get too high or too low, people said. If you had the ability to hide your emotions, you could detach from the outcome and move on to the next practice, game, or team without snags. Professional athletes are trained to desensitize our feelings in order to stay focused. We're taught to put everything into the team, even at the expense of our own well-being.

But this wasn't truly the best option. I learned that the ability to show and share your emotions will help you reach your destination of becoming truly elite. As I always share with men, "Vulnerability equals masculinity."

I hope this background gives you some context into what the four proven pillars are about and how they impact your overall life each day. With that being said, I realized with each new layer of discovery within my own journey, it brought to the surface the separate ways we are all impacted.

For example, in my book *Becoming Elite*, I talk about how definitions enable us to have a mutual understanding of a word or subject. They allow us to all be on the same page when discussing or reading about an issue or topic. Having a foundational vocabulary is imperative to helping you implement the 1% impact you want in your life. Comprehending the definition of a word drastically improves your understanding of how it applies to your life.

There are many words that have slightly different meanings to different people. In each section of this book, I examine a different pair of closely-related words that seem similar, but may have a slightly different overall meaning to you than they do to me. And guess what? That's okay.

But the next level of understanding is, how do *you* react each day, each moment, and within each new interaction? We all have a different understanding of what we want and what helps us get the most out of our 1%. The impact is often through small, incremental changes that can have a significant cumulative effect over time.

Think about it this way: if you save 1% of your income each month, the compounding effect over time will significantly grow your wealth. For example, let's assume you have an initial monthly income of $5,000 and you save 1% of your income per month, which means $50 per month. Let's take the average annual interest rate of 5% on the money you save. Using a formula to calculate the future value over a 20-year time period, your savings would grow to approximately $20,637. This demonstrates how small, consistent savings can compound and grow over time.

Similarly, adding just 1% more time and effort to your daily workout, such as one more minute of running or one more set of weight lifting, can gradually improve your physical fitness and health. This is also true for boosting your business's profitability over time by improving customer satisfaction by 1% each day, which leads to higher retention rates. These examples show that even those small, consistent behaviors lead to extraordinary outcomes, and this can look different for everyone.

In fact, that is the purpose of this book: to dig deeper into what's holding you back, to get you to think outside the box and step out on the other side with the ability to become a better version of you by committing to the 1% impact every day. This is about you, not me. This is your chance to step into the unknown, push yourself to new limits, and figure out how you can level up 1% at a time.

All of us have a past, and it is important to be able to embrace your past before preparing to evaluate your current self against what you want your future self to look like. Our past provides us with a roadmap to what has worked and what hasn't worked in our lives. Once we establish and accept that the past cannot be altered, we then need to understand that we can't repeat our negative behaviors and expect positive change in our lives.

The ability to stay present while being able to visualize your future in a positive light can be advantageous. The same is true if you are able to look at your past as a learning experience, not a loss. This involves framing failures or past losses in a positive light as something you learned from that specific experience or outcome. We learn from both our successes and our failures. This is true in sports, business, and life. Once you learn to establish a sense of appreciation and acknowledgement for your past, it increases your ability to direct your future.

So, what are you waiting for? It's time to get off the bench and into the game and make the 1% impact in your life that you've been waiting for. Let's go!

## Current Self vs. Future Self

The present moment affects both your current and your future self. It's a balancing act. How do we decide what is the right or wrong thing to do? What should we focus on to level up today and impact tomorrow? Our lives are a constant interplay between who we are now (present self) and who we aspire to be (future self). These selves can sometimes feel at odds, with our present self craving instant gratification and our future self yearning for long-term success. This predicament can feel like a dance between who we are now and who we could be. Understanding this dynamic is crucial for making choices that benefit both versions of ourselves.

I struggled with this comparison as I got older and stepped out of the shadow of being a professional hockey player. As I transitioned from being a hockey player my entire life to a regular civilian, it wasn't easy to know which way to turn. In hockey or any sport, players are judged by statistics: how many goals, assists, points, wins, losses, and so on. The pressure you put on yourself sometimes can seem insurmountable, and this pressure on top of the expectations of your team and fans can take you into a dark place. In fact, former sports professionals frequently suffer from negative life events post-retirement: depression, bankruptcy, addiction, divorce, or a combination.

Statistics around professional athletes and retirement
(combined statistical research)

| Addiction | Bankruptcy | Depression | Divorce |
| --- | --- | --- | --- |
| 52% - 67% experience some kind of addiction | 78% go broke within 3 years of retirement | 39% suffer from depression after retirement | 60% - 80% get divorced during retirement |

This is because we don't look at how our current situation and actions will affect our future self. We are so focused on the present that we forget about the future. This is true throughout every stage of life. In middle school you can't wait to get to high school. When you're in high school, you are asked where you want to go to college and what you want to become. In college you're expected to know where you want to be in five years and what you want to do for the rest of your life. And the cycle continues until you feel overwhelmed or worse yet, spiral into depression, experience a divorce, hit rock bottom with an addiction, or lose all your money.

I'm here to tell you that doesn't have to be the case. My dad always used to quote Eleanor Roosevelt: "Yesterday is history. Tomorrow's a mystery. Today is a gift. That's why we call it the present." The quote suggests focusing too much on the future can cause people to miss out on the present. This is true, but it also helps when you have the ability to follow your plan today in order to help you achieve your goals for tomorrow. By living your purpose today, you will instill confidence to grow and achieve even more success tomorrow.

The key to seeing the correlation between your current self and your future self is in the theory of cause and effect. The cause is the initiating event or situation, and the effect is the result of the cause. The daily actions taken by your current self are shaping your future self each day. If you take a shortcut today, it could have a long-term effect on you in the future.

## The Present Self: Instant Gratification and Short-Term Focus

The present self is all about the here and now. It craves instant gratification and prioritizes experiences and desires in the immediate moment. This can be a great motivator, pushing us to enjoy life and seize opportunities. However, the present self can also lead us to prioritize short-term pleasures over long-term goals. We might choose to indulge in an unhealthy snack instead of sticking to a healthy diet or hit the snooze button instead of getting up for a workout. The present self is also susceptible to temporal discounting, meaning the further away a reward is, the less valuable it seems. This makes saving for retirement or a big purchase feel less appealing than indulging in something fun today. More than 65% of us can only guess when we will retire and what we'll need when that day eventually comes.

## The Future Self: Long-Term Vision and Delayed Rewards

The future self, on the other hand, is concerned with the bigger picture. It considers the long-term consequences of our actions and motivates us to work towards our aspirations and expand more into the unknown. The future self might remind us of the health benefits of sticking to a diet or the importance of exercise for our future well-being. It prioritizes delayed rewards and making sacrifices now for a better future. The future self might envision a healthier lifestyle, financial security, or a fulfilling career. However, the future self lacks immediate influence and can often be overshadowed by the desires of the present self. This can feel like an internal tug-of-war, with our desire for instant gratification battling against our long-term goals.

## The Present Self

- Focused on the here and now.
- Driven by emotions and immediate desires.
- Prone to impulsive decisions and instant gratification.
- May prioritize comfort and pleasure over long-term goals.

### The Future Self

- Represents your aspirations and goals.
- Concerned with the long-term consequences of your actions.
- Motivated by a vision of your ideal future.
- Values delayed gratification and self-discipline.

### The Battle Within: Bridging the Gap

The present self and future self often have conflicting desires and see you differently depending on your focus. This internal struggle can lead to procrastination, unhealthy habits, and a feeling of being stuck. However, by consciously considering your future self, you can bridge this gap and make choices that benefit you in the long run. Here are some strategies to help your present self take better care of your future self:

- **Visualize your future self:** Spend some time imagining your ideal future. What does your life look like? Who are you? Having a clear vision can motivate you to make choices that align with those goals. It is important to take time to visualize your future self and what your ideal life looks like. This can make long-term goals feel more real and motivating.

- **Goal Setting:** Set SMART goals (Specific, Measurable, Achievable, Relevant, and Timely) for your future self. Breaking down large goals into smaller, achievable steps makes them feel less daunting for the present self. I will come back to this often in the chapters ahead. You can also find tools to implement and execute more quickly at www.erikwestrumbook.com.

- **Commitment Devices:** Utilize commitment devices to "lock yourself in" to positive choices. This could involve putting money away automatically, scheduling workouts in advance, or telling a friend about a goal to hold yourself accountable. Make choices now that will benefit your future self later. For example, I wear my gym clothes to bed with my socks in my pocket so when I get out of bed, I'm ready to go (yes, my wife thinks I'm crazy). If you want to take that dream vacation, you can start setting aside money for that future experience.

- **Focus on Progress, Not Perfection:** Don't get discouraged by setbacks. Focus on making progress, not achieving perfection. Celebrating small wins can keep you motivated along the way. Positive reinforcement goes a long way. Find ways to reward yourself for making choices that benefit your future self. I talk about this in the 3 Daily Tools section of my first book, *Becoming Elite*, and how you need to celebrate the wins in your Nightly Pulse (visit www.erikwestrumbook.com for the 3 Daily Tools, the 5-Minute Nightly Pulse, the 10-Minute Daily Check-in, and the Mid-Day Recalibration).

A great example of focusing on progress is when you are trying to write a book. You don't even need to write a full page, let alone a full chapter, to make progress. You also don't need to go back and reread every word, paragraph, and chapter you write. Instead, commit to writing 15 minutes a day, and after 30 days you'll be surprised at how close your book will be to the finish line. Each day, celebrate the small step forward and enjoy the process.

This can also be seen in losing weight or gaining muscle mass. If you put in 15 minutes per day to address the goal by doing the work, celebrating the win, and enjoying the progress, you'll see the results in no time. Just remind yourself that it takes work, even when no one is looking. It's not about perfection, but all about making progress 1% at a time.

By understanding the present self vs. future self dynamic and employing these strategies, you can make choices that create a smoother path towards your goals and a future self you'll be proud of. Remember, your future self is counting on you—make choices today that your future self will thank you for, but also live in the moment. That's the beauty of the balancing act we face each day. It only takes 15 minutes a day to make a difference and inspire you to believe in yourself 1% at a time.

## If You Believe, You Will Achieve

"If you believe, you will achieve" is a popular motivational quote from Napoleon Hill, but it's important to understand its limitations. A big buzz word people often use is "manifest." Yes, it's important to manifest your future, but it's one thing to say it and another thing to do it or make strides towards the desired outcome. Just think of how powerful the mind is when you look at these two quotes and decide which one fits your mindset:

"If you can believe, then you will achieve."

"If you can't believe, then you can't achieve."

Let the power of each of those quotes sink in. The belief you have in yourself will 99% of the time dictate the direction and outcome of your life. It's a choice we all have, but unfortunately the majority of us don't have the mindset to choose the first quote. You have to look at yourself in the mirror and ask, What do I choose to do today in order to impact my tomorrow? It only takes a 1% commitment to transform your belief.

## The Power of Belief

- Belief can be a powerful force. It fosters confidence, increases resilience, and fuels motivation.

- Believing in yourself and your abilities can help you overcome challenges and push yourself further.

## Limitations of Belief

- Belief alone isn't enough. For significant achievements, you need to combine belief with:
    - **Action:** Just believing in your dream won't make it happen. You need to take concrete steps to turn your vision into reality.

- **Planning and Strategy:** A clear plan and effective strategies are crucial for navigating challenges and obstacles.

- **Hard Work and Persistence:** Success rarely comes easily. Be prepared to put in the challenging work and persevere through setbacks.

It's not as simple as just believing. You need to look at how you can turn believing into achieving. If you believe in yourself, plan effectively, work hard, and persist, you will increase your chances of achieving your goals.

## How do we find a more balanced approach to make an impact of 1% at a time?

Yes, you need to take action. You can't just sit on the sidelines or on the couch and expect the results to come. Instead, stand up, speak up, and take one step at a time to make an impact in your life today.

What's holding you back? Do you need more motivation and inspiration from those who have forged the way? Here are some quotes that capture a more nuanced perspective on achievement:

- Vince Lombardi emphasized the importance of hard work when he said, "The difference between successful people and others is not a lack of strength, not a lack of knowledge, but rather a lack of will."

- Marion Wright Edelman highlighted the power of belief combined with action when he said, "Success is most often achieved by those who don't know it is impossible."

- Michael Jordan focused on resiliency and persistence when he said, "I've missed more than 9000 shots in my career. I've lost almost 300 games. Twenty-six times, I've been trusted to take the game winning shot and missed. I've failed over and over and over again in my life. And that is why I succeed."

- Finally, my all-time favorite hockey player, Wayne Gretzky, emphasized the importance of taking chances when he said, "You miss 100% of the shots you don't take." So why not keep shooting?

That's why believing in yourself is a great first step, but you shouldn't underestimate the power of dedicated effort and a well-defined plan. You need to make it a top priority in your life if you want to reap the rewards.

My neighbor patiently plants trees, waters them, protects them from critters, and gives them tender loving care. My kids reap the benefits in the delicious fruit he brings over to them throughout the year. I told a friend of mine, "Man, I wish I had those apple and pear trees in my yard, but I don't know anything about picking a weed, let alone planting a tree. I don't even know when a good time to plant them would be."

As we both laughed, he said, "Westy, that's easy. Today is the right time. What you plant today, you reap tomorrow."

This has impacted and inspired me each day to make an impact. Galatians 5:22-23 reads, "But the fruit of the Spirit is love, joy, peace, patience, kindness, goodness, faithfulness, gentleness and self-control." Step outside of your comfort zone and plant that tree so you can reap the rewards and enjoy the fruit in your life.

As you recite the quote, "If you believe, you will achieve," notice the positive energy it fills you with. It can impact your life on various levels, but it isn't enough all on its own.

**Pros**

- **Belief fosters confidence:** Believing in yourself and your abilities can be a powerful motivator. It fuels the confidence you need to take on challenges and persist through setbacks.

- **Positive self-fulfilling prophecy:** When you believe you can achieve something, you're more likely to put in the effort and focus needed to make it happen. Your belief shapes your actions and behaviors.

- **Opens you to possibilities:** Believing in possibilities can spark creativity and help you explore options you might otherwise dismiss.

**Cons**

- **Oversimplification of success:** Achievement often requires more than just belief. Factors like skill, hard work, resources, and external circumstances also play a role.

- **Discourages planning and action:** Solely focusing on belief can lead to neglecting the importance of planning, acquiring necessary skills, and taking concrete steps toward your goals.

## A More Balanced Approach

Make sure you have a good understanding of how to incorporate moderation into the equation and create your individualized plan.

- **Pair Belief with Action:** Combine your belief with dedicated effort, strategizing, and continuous learning. In sports, work, and life, it's this combination that turns the thought into a reality.

- **Embrace Flexibility:** Believing in your ability to adapt and overcome obstacles is key. Things don't always go according to plan, so adjust your approach as needed. I didn't always do this in my life. I'd usually blame others if something didn't go as planned instead of looking at myself and evaluating what I could do.

- **Celebrate Small Wins:** Acknowledge and celebrate your progress along the way. This reinforces your belief in your abilities and keeps you motivated. I learned this lesson from my friend PJ Fleck in how he approaches celebrating both the big and small wins in life.

Belief is a powerful tool, but it's most effective when combined with planning, effort, and a willingness to learn and adapt. Now it's time for you to make a change in how you approach your day, your life, and your belief in yourself. There is no better time than the present to take control of your today in order to impact your tomorrow, 1% at a time. Let's go!

## Confidence vs. Humility

Confidence and humility, while seemingly opposite ends of a spectrum, are actually two sides of the same coin when it comes to personal growth and achievement. The seemingly opposite traits are both valuable and can even coexist in a healthy way. The important distinction is how each of the traits show up and how you approach them with authenticity.

### Confidence

- Belief in your abilities and skills. Belief in *you*.

- A healthy sense of self-worth and respect. Having a positive self-image and feeling self-assured.

- Confidence allows you to take risks, pursue goals, and navigate challenges while increasing your feelings of empowerment.

- Excessive confidence can morph into arrogance, leading to disrespect for others and an inflated sense of self-importance. Need to find balance.

**Humility**

- An awareness of your limitations and a willingness to learn from others. A realistic understanding of one's strengths and weaknesses.

- Not boastful or arrogant about your achievements. Openness to learning and personal growth.

- Receptive to criticism and willing to learn and grow. Ability to acknowledge the contributions of others. It is also important to be open to feedback.

- Excessive humility can lead to downplaying your strengths and hinder you from reaching your full potential. Humility can turn into self-deprecation if not balanced with confidence.

It's easy to see the interplay between confidence and humility and how important it is to understand how they both shape you. So how do you find the sweet spot of being confident while being humble?

### The Sweet Spot: Confident Humility

The ideal state is often referred to as *confident humility*. This is when you believe in yourself and your abilities, but also recognize your limitations and are open to learning. Here are some characteristics of confident humility:

- **Realistic self-assessment:** Having self-awareness to know and reflect on your strengths and weaknesses and be honest with yourself.

- **Willingness to learn:** You should always be open to new information and experiences. Continue to embrace lifelong learning by seeking opportunities to learn and grow.

- **Collaboration:** You value the contributions of others and work effectively with them. By appreciating others, you can recognize the talents and contributions of those around you.

- **Inspiring leadership:** You motivate others with your confidence while remaining approachable and humble.

As a young hockey player, I learned that in order to survive and thrive, I needed to have confidence to make it to the highest level year after year. It was a challenge to learn when to turn it off and be humble. As I got older, it became easier to delineate between being confident but not coming across as arrogant. At the same time, I came to understand that you don't want or have to lose your confidence and swagger to move into being humble. Otherwise, you slip into the trap of complacency while blaming others for the outcome instead of standing tall and taking control.

## Why They Both Matter

Both confidence and humility are crucial for success and positive relationships. Confidence allows you to take action and pursue your goals, while humility fosters growth and collaboration. By striking a balance between the two, you can achieve a sense of confident humility that will empower you to reach your full potential. I've seen this firsthand running businesses as well as working for others. You need to be relational as well as transactional in showing you have the confidence to lead, but also be humble enough to delegate in order to help others to elevate.

## The Synergy Effect

Implementing synergy is crucial for achieving better outcomes in various contexts, such as business, teams, and personal projects. This is how you can use synergy to transform individual contributions into greater collective success and achieve extraordinary results.

- **True confidence stems from humility.** When you understand your limitations, you're more likely to seek out knowledge, improve your skills, and appreciate the expertise of others. This grounded confidence inspires growth and fosters collaboration.

- **Humility strengthens confidence.** By being open to feedback and learning from others, you can continuously improve and refine your abilities. This reinforces your confidence and expands your skillset.

## Benefits of the Balance

Maintaining balance in life is key to overall well-being and fulfillment. Here are some of the primary benefits:

- **Improved decision-making:** A blend of confidence and humility allows you to weigh your own ideas alongside others', leading to more informed choices.

- **Stronger relationships:** When you acknowledge the strengths of others and avoid arrogance, you build trust and foster collaboration.

- **Greater resilience:** Humility allows you to learn from setbacks and bounce back stronger, while confidence fuels your determination.

- **Openness to new experiences:** Confidence pushes you to step outside your comfort zone, while humility allows you to approach challenges with a learning mindset.

By cultivating both confidence and humility, you can develop a solid foundation for personal growth, effective leadership, and fulfilling relationships. It's not about being all one or the other, but rather finding the sweet spot where these two qualities work together to propel you forward. Often there's a fine line between confidence and arrogance, just like there's a fine line between humility and self-deprecation. You need to be confident, but not at the expense of sacrificing your humility.

It's also important to realize that arrogance can lead to a lonely journey and make you into someone that others don't want to be around. The slow downward spiral can turn quickly from confidence to arrogance and, from there, into self-deprecation. This will only turn you upside down in what you are trying to accomplish in life.

Yes, you should want to grow in confidence, but not at the expense of others, and definitely not at the cost of losing yourself. This is why, if you focus on cultivating confident humility, you can achieve a powerful combination that will propel you forward in life.

I remember the first time I met my wife and her initial thoughts on who I was: a cocky, overconfident jerk.

Why?

Because I showed up as the hockey player I had trained myself to be and not the person I truly was behind the mask. This was a perfect example of how confidence can be perceived as egotistical. Fast forward a few months to our first real conversation where we connected on a personal level. If you ask about that moment, she'll tell you how kind, nice, and caring I was when we sat and talked. That was the first time I showed up as the version of me who knew humility and had an openness to learn more about her.

The example with my wife can easily translate to any part of life. Just think about your first interview with a new company and how you showed up. On the flip side, if you're the interviewer instead, how do you show up? Depending on what side of the coin you are on, you will show up differently.

I've learned that no matter who you are with and what you are trying to achieve, you need a balance of confidence and humility. But what is the right mix? The beautiful thing is that we all have a different balance of confidence and humility that will make us successful in life. You need to lean into what you trust and who you want to be. This makes the difference in finding out how you will show up when no one's looking.

# The 1% Impact – Transform Your Life Worksheet

What can you do today that will impact your future self tomorrow?

_____
_____
_____
_____

What do you believe you can achieve in the next 2 days, 2 months, or 2 years?

_____
_____
_____
_____

When do you have the most confidence?

_____
_____
_____
_____
_____

# WHO

The journey is about you.

The impact you can make today.

The influence you can have on others.

The foundation you develop as you grow.

# Reliability vs. Stability

I've always had a hard time accepting how reliability and stability actually impacted my life. It wasn't so much the lack of these elements in my life, but more so the development of the self-awareness to realize how they affected me. Reliability and stability provide a foundation of trust and security for me to fall back on that allow me to navigate challenges with confidence and consistency. When these are present, you can foster stronger relationships, personal growth, and long-term success, creating a sense of balance in both your personal and professional life.

Only you know how you show up every day and who you are in life. Ask yourself, "Am I reliable?" and "Do I have stability in my life?" It's one thing to answer the questions with a "yes," but another to actually live it. Most people think they are reliable until they take a deeper look at how they actually show up. We can all be better, but we need to realize it starts with us.

One way to work on this daily is by utilizing positive self-talk, 15 minutes per day. Ask yourself if you're worth an extra 1% effort to improve your life. The more you tell yourself how great you are and what you want to accomplish, the more it will slowly become a reality. Self-talk plays a crucial role in shaping our mindset, influencing our emotions, and guiding our actions. Positive self-talk can boost confidence, reduce stress, and enhance resilience, while negative self-talk can undermine our self-esteem and limit our potential for growth and success.

The same is true for the concept of having stability, but most people don't even think they have stability. That's why they are always trying to achieve more. More money equals more stability. More success equals more stability. And the cycle never stops, as most people never feel like they are truly living a stable life.

We all have the opportunity to change the narrative and show up more authentically on both sides of the coin. Let's take a look at the slight but noticeable differences between reliability and stability.

**Reliability**

- The consistency of a system or process in performing its function as expected.

- A reliable system produces accurate and dependable results over time.

- Examples: A reliable car starts every time; a reliable friend is always there for you.

**Stability**

- The ability of a system or process to maintain its state or function even during disruptions or changes.

- A stable system is resistant to errors and fluctuations.

- Examples: A stable economy experiences steady growth; a stable person remains calm under pressure.

The first part of the process is being reliable no matter what. This sets you apart from the crowd and increases your chance of being successful. It also springboards you into having more stability in order to drive yourself to a fulfilling life of purpose. I've found this true with showing up consistently for my kids. If you honor your commitments and keep your promises, you'll gain the trust of those around you. If you maintain this consistently, you'll have more stability in your life, your relationships, and your ability to grow personally.

A simple example is when my kids ask me to help them with something or do something with them. If I tell them that I'll do it, but I don't follow through, what message am I sending them? This happens a lot to people with busy lives—our words say yes, but our actions say no.

As the saying goes, you can be reliable 364 days of the year, but the one day you don't show up will be the one day someone's watching. This doesn't mean you need to be perfect, but it does mean you need to be aware of how you show up when you commit to someone or something. This is on you. You are in control.

## The Relationship Between Reliability and Stability

While there is a connection between the two, they are not identical. A system can be reliable but not necessarily stable. For instance, a complex machine might function perfectly under normal conditions (reliable), but malfunction when faced with unexpected stress (not stable). Conversely, a system can be stable but not perfectly reliable. For example, a simple system with redundancies might rarely fail entirely (stable) but may have occasional errors (not perfectly reliable).

## The Importance of Both

Both reliability and stability are crucial depending on the context. In safety-critical systems, like airplanes or medical devices, reliability is paramount. Even a minor malfunction can have catastrophic consequences. In systems designed to handle changing environments, stability becomes more important. For instance, an ecosystem needs to be stable to adapt to gradual changes.

Reliability and stability are complementary concepts contributing to the overall effectiveness of a larger system. Understanding the distinction between them allows us to design and evaluate systems for optimal performance in different situations. This is not only true in business but also in life. Again, look at the side-by-side comparison of how they differ but yet are so closely related to how you approach life.

| Feature | Reliability | Stability |
|---|---|---|
| Definition | Consistency of a system or process in performing its function as expected. | Ability of a system or process to maintain its state or function even during disruptions or changes. |

| | | |
|---|---|---|
| Example | A reliable car starts every time. | A stable economy experiences steady growth. |
| Importance | Crucial in safety-critical systems. | Crucial in systems designed to handle changing environments. |

When you focus on having both reliability and stability in your life, you'll find that it's easier to increase the rate at which you accomplish your goals. Try to show up on time and fulfill every commitment you make over the course of a year. This will change your life. Now, add in the stability of your mind to overcome the desire to take the easy way out. The discipline you will slowly instill will pay dividends in your life, work, and overall well-being.

If I wasn't reliable in my own life, how could I expect others to know I'd be reliable in their lives? That was a hard but important lesson to learn. It's invaluable to make the changes needed in order to show up consistently in your life, because it helps add joy, peace, and love on a daily basis.

As I wrote this chapter, it was a beautiful, sunny spring day, and a lovely yellow bird came to my window. I'm not sure why, but I looked up the meaning of yellow birds and realized the timing of it was no coincidence. The first thing that popped up on Google was, "Yellow birds often symbolize joy, positivity, and the energy of life due to their bright coloration, which is associated with the sun… In many cultures, seeing a yellow bird is considered a sign of good luck and an indicator of upcoming positive change."

I believe this yellow bird came to me for a reason: so I could tell you that life is full of possibilities, but before you can find them, you need to look at yourself and answer these two questions: are you reliable, and are you stable in your life today?

We all have it in us to be better, and it only takes 1% to impact your life in a positive way. Can you do it consistently, or are you complacent in your life today? Let's find out.

## 1% Impact:
## One Thing You Can Do Today to be More Reliable

Follow through on one promise or commitment.

- Identify a promise or commitment that you've made to someone (or yourself) and ensure you complete it today.

Examples: respond to an email message you've been putting off, show up on time for an appointment or meeting, or finish a task or chore you said you'd do.

*Check it off your list and celebrate the WIN!*

***Why it Matters:*** Reliability and stability are built through consistent follow-through. Completing even one commitment today strengthens your trustworthiness and reinforces the habit of honoring your word.

### FREE GIFT:
### BONUS TRAINING To Become More Reliable and Stable in Your Life

Are you tired of not following through on your promises and want to learn how to master three simple keys to help you create a foundation of trustworthiness and stability? Then my free training will help serve both you and those around you. You can watch it at:

erikwestrumbook.com/training, or scan the QR code on the next page to go directly to the free training.

## Bookmark This Page!

Scan this QR code after each section of the book for direct access to FREE training modules to enhance your learning and growth.

## Complacency vs. Consistency

Complacency and consistency, while sometimes confused with each other, represent opposite ends of a spectrum. I had a tough time admitting I needed to find complacency within the busy chaos of my life, but it was important to do so in order to reset and not burn out. Mind you, this didn't mean I wasn't driven to achieve the next "big thing," or I was settling for less. Instead, it meant I had the opportunity to be complacent with what I had accomplished while resetting to start my next journey in life.

A perfect example is when I made it to the NHL, and the following year we had a league-wide lockout. This meant the NHL did not play the entire 2004-2005 season, so I decided to sign in the AHL to at least have an opportunity to play. Instead of striving to get better, I was complacent about the fact that I had already made it to the "big leagues." Yes, this was a chance to reset, but it also could have been a dangerous turning point of not striving for more the next year.

That is why it's important to know how moving 1% in the right direction can change your trajectory one day at a time. Let's break down the key differences between these concepts:

### Complacency

- A state of satisfaction or contentment that can lead to a lack of motivation or drive.

- Settling for the status quo.

- Resistance to change or improvement.

- Neglecting goals or responsibilities.

- Feeling a lack of urgency or purpose.

**Consistency**

- Steadfast adherence to a course of action or principle.

- Regularly taking action towards goals.

- Maintaining routines and habits.

- Adapting and improving upon existing approaches.

- Demonstrating discipline and commitment.

A drastic difference can fool you by creating a sense of disorientation or surprise, causing you to focus on the most apparent change while overlooking other crucial details. As we say in the book publishing world, don't judge a book by its cover, but instead dig deeper into the impact both complacency and consistency have on you.

**Complacency** leads to stagnation and hinders progress. It can erode skills and make it harder to adapt to new challenges. **Consistency** breeds success by fostering progress and improvement. It allows you to build upon your skills and knowledge over time.

## The Balancing Act

While consistency is generally desirable, it's important to avoid rigid consistency. This often involves clinging to outdated methods or failing to adapt to changing circumstances. The ideal approach is *flexible consistency*. This means maintaining a commitment to your goals and habits while also being open to adjustments as needed. This is where temporary complacency happens in order to reset and reevaluate what is next.

While consistency is crucial for achieving goals, a dash of healthy dissatisfaction can be a good thing. Here's why:

- **Complacency as a Signal:** Sometimes, a period of complacency can be a signal that your goals need reassessment. Are they still challenging and motivating?

- **Striving for Progress, Not Perfection:** Consistency is about progress, not perfection. Allowing yourself some flexibility can prevent burnout and keep you motivated overall.

## Strategies for Embracing Flexible Consistency

- Regularly evaluate your goals and progress.
- Be open to learning new skills or approaches.

- Celebrate small wins as you move forward.

- Forgive yourself for occasional setbacks and get back on track.

Remember, complacency is a comfort zone that leads to stagnation. Consistency is the key to continual progress and achieving your goals. By embracing flexible consistency, you can maintain the dedication required for success while also being adaptable enough to navigate the inevitable changes that life throws your way. This is where *self-awareness* comes into play in our lives to help us truly grow. Self-awareness involves being aware of various aspects of the self, including traits, behaviors, and feelings.

It is important to utilize a tool of self-reflection to see who you are, where you are succeeding, and where you can improve. The ability to get closer to self-mastery starts with being vulnerable, open, and honest with yourself. This is a challenge for everyone, and it cannot be bought, only taught. It requires consistency and grit. It's a daily battle, which means it's not easy. But if you never quit, never give up, never give in, you can learn to master yourself. Here are some tips to consider when looking at yourself.

### Tips for Avoiding Complacency and Embracing Consistency

- **Set SMART goals:** Specific, Measurable, Achievable, Relevant, and Time-bound goals provide a clear roadmap for your efforts. You need goals to keep you on track and headed in the right direction. Start with simple goals to keep you motivated by having initial success. This is as easy as walking each morning for 15 minutes or reading 10 pages of a book each day. This gives you a sense of accomplishment, which keeps you moving in the right direction.

- **Track your progress:** Monitor your progress to stay motivated and identify areas for improvement. If you're not tracking what you're doing, how do you know what is working and what you need to change? It only takes 1% improvement at a time to make an impact and keep the momentum to reach your next level of success.

- **Celebrate milestones:** Acknowledge and reward yourself for achieving milestones to maintain momentum. I always say how important it is to celebrate the successes in your life.

- **Seek out challenges:** Step outside your comfort zone and embrace new challenges to keep things interesting. When you start to get uncomfortable, that is when you truly know that you're growing.

- **Find an accountability partner:** Having someone to support and motivate you can be a powerful tool. Get an accountability partner and commit to making a change.

By understanding the differences between complacency and consistency, you can cultivate the right mindset and habits needed to achieve lasting success in your endeavors. It's consistent effort, not just occasional bursts of motivation, that leads to real progress.

Here is an easy example I use with the student athletes I coach and train, highlighting how the simple choice between two words can drastically change the outcome:

- **Complacency:** An athlete who stops training after an initial win. This will lead to continued failure.

- **Consistency:** A student who studies regularly to maintain good grades. This will lead to continued opportunities for success.

## From Complacency to Consistency

- **Develop Self-Awareness:** Recognizing the signs of complacency is the first step towards change.

- **Set SMART Goals:** Specific, Measurable, Achievable, Relevant, and Time-bound goals provide direction and motivation.

- **Celebrate Milestones:** Acknowledging progress keeps you engaged and motivated.

- **Seek Continuous Improvement:** Always look for ways to learn and grow.

The power is felt when you move from complacency to consistency on a regular basis. Consistency is not about achieving perfection; it's about steady and dependable effort. By consistently working towards your goals, you develop the skills and discipline needed for long-term success. Small, consistent steps lead to considerable progress over time. If you add 1% to your life each day for the next 100 days, you've just made a 100% transformation. Pretty easy, sure, yet still pretty remarkable.

## 1% Impact:
## One Thing You Can Do Today to be More Consistent

Set a small, specific goal, and complete it.

- Choosing one simple, actionable task that aligns with your priorities and commit to completing it by the end of the day.

Examples: drink 8 glasses of water if you're working on health goals, write 100 words if you're working on a writing habit, or spend 5 minutes organizing if productivity is a focus.

***Check it off your list and celebrate the WIN!***

**Why it Matters:** Consistency is built by starting small and showing up daily. Completing one specific task today reinforces the habit of taking regular action, no matter how small, toward your goal.

## FREE GIFT:
## TRAINING on How to Be Consistent EVERY DAY

Question: When was the last time you were consistent in something in your life? The result was most likely success. I've created a free training for you to implement the steps to become more consistent in your life by starting small, building systems, and embracing accountability. Then you can achieve greater consistency and, ultimately, long-term success. You can watch it free at:

erikwestrumbook.com/training, or scan the QR code

# Collaboration vs. Competition

My third year playing professional hockey took place in 2003, and I was still trying to crack the NHL roster on a regular basis. It was January 2004, and I had just gotten called up for the second half of the season. As I arrived to watch our team play that night, I wanted nothing more than for them to lose.

Why?

Because with yet another loss, I knew I'd be getting in the lineup as they looked to change things up. They lost. Following the game, I was told I would be playing my first NHL game the next day. This was going to be a dream come true and the moment I had been working so hard to accomplish ever since I was a young boy.

Instead, our coach got fired, and I was on the next plane back to the minors. That was not what I had been hoping for, and it meant I had a choice to make: collaborate with my teammates, or be selfish?

I knew from past experience that every time I had chosen selfishness over collaborating with others, I had failed. So, for three weeks I collaborated with my teammates, competing together for a successful second half of our minor league season. With that collaboration came the call I was waiting for. I was going to play in my first NHL hockey game on March 7, 2004. It was a dream come true.

Collaboration and competition are two driving forces that can play out in various aspects of life, from business to sports to personal development. While they may seem like opposites, they both have their merits and can even be used together strategically. This is the part I didn't realize until later in life as I reflected on all the individual and team success I had had. The common theme was elite collaboration with elite competition. All of the championships and scoring titles happened when I was 100% bought into the team and excelled through the competition.

Let's take a look at collaboration and competition to see how they both affect you daily.

**Collaboration**

- **Definition:** Working together to achieve a common goal.

- **Synergy:** Combining skills, knowledge, and perspectives leads to better solutions.

- **Shared Motivation:** Teamwork fosters a sense of community and shared responsibility, boosting morale and motivation.

- **Efficiency:** Dividing tasks and leveraging each other's strengths can save time and resources. Utilize everyone's ability to level up 1% at a time.

- **Examples:** Teamwork in sports, scientific research collaborations, brainstorming sessions.

## Competition

- **Definition:** Striving to outperform others to achieve a goal.

- **Motivation:** Competition can drive individuals and teams to push their limits and achieve excellence. Human beings need to be pushed outside their comfort zones to become elite and go above and beyond 1% each day.

- **Innovation:** A competitive environment can spark creativity and innovation as people strive to gain an edge. This is what we call healthy competition in life, sports, and business.

- **Benchmarking:** Evaluating yourself against competitors helps identify areas for improvement. Track it. Measure it. Execute it.

- **Examples:** Business competition, athletic events, academic competitions.

## Finding the Right Balance

The ideal approach often involves finding the right balance between collaboration and competition. Here's how they can complement each other:

- **Healthy Competition within Collaboration:** Teams can compete internally for sub-goals while still collaborating towards a shared objective. This is what helped me in hockey and business.

- **Learning from the Competition:** Studying successful competitors can inspire innovation and improvement within your own team. Knowledge is key to success.

- **Collaboration after Competition:** Even competitors can collaborate after a contest, for example, by sharing knowledge or developing industry standards.

The best personal approach to using collaboration and competition depends on the specific context. We all have separate ways to add 1% to our lives and achieve our goals. You need to find out what is best for you in order to have the greatest chance at success. Here are some factors to consider:

- **Nature of the Goal:** Is it a project requiring diverse expertise (collaboration) or a race to a single solution (competition)?

- **Team Dynamics:** Do team members work well together, or would a competitive environment bring out the best in them? This is a huge balancing act in sports the higher up you go. This is also true when balancing an in-person vs. remote working environment.

- **External Landscape:** Is there a strong competitive environment, or is collaboration more beneficial for the industry as a whole?

Collaboration and competition are not mutually exclusive forces. By understanding their advantages, you can leverage them strategically to achieve success, whether you are working towards a personal goal, in a team environment, or even within a competitive industry.

## The Advantages of Collaboration

Collaboration offers numerous advantages in various contexts, from business environments to personal projects.

- **Enhanced Problem Solving:** Diverse perspectives lead to more creative and effective solutions.

- **Increased Efficiency:** Teamwork allows for division of labor and faster completion of tasks.

- **Stronger Relationships:** Collaboration fosters trust and communication, leading to a more positive work environment.

## The Advantages of Competition

Competition is usually linked to sports but can also be connected to business, education, and personal development.

- **Improved Performance:** Competition can push individuals and teams to perform at their best.

- **Goal Setting and Tracking:** Competition provides a clear benchmark for measuring progress.

- **Increased Adaptability:** A competitive environment can help teams adapt to changing market demands.

By understanding the strengths and weaknesses of both collaboration and competition, you can choose the best approach to achieve your goals and maximize your potential.

## The Ideal Scenario: Collaborative Competition

The most successful environments utilize a blend of collaboration and competition, sometimes referred to as collaborative competition. Here's how they work together:

- **Collaborative Competition:** Teams compete with each other, but also share knowledge and resources to achieve a common goal (e.g., inter-departmental sales competitions)

- **Healthy Rivalry:** Fostering a competitive spirit within a team environment can motivate individuals without sacrificing collaboration.

Teams can work together to achieve a common goal, but there's still an element of competition, perhaps with other teams or against a set benchmark. This fosters a sense of camaraderie and shared purpose while still motivating individuals and teams to excel. The goal is to find a happy medium, though you may find more or less collaboration or competition is helpful depending on the situation you face.

## When to Choose Collaboration or Competition

- **Collaboration is ideal:** When complex problems require diverse perspectives, and solutions need to be creative and innovative.

- **Competition is ideal:** When individual motivation and a drive to outperform are crucial for success.

By understanding the strengths and weaknesses of both collaboration and competition, you can create an environment that fosters creativity, motivation, and ultimately, success. This is the key to finding the true north star of your personal and professional journey toward becoming elite. The ability to identify the 1% impact both collaboration and competition can have on your life is game changing. Even better, it's easy to put into play. Just make an effort to reach outside your comfort zone 1% at a time and watch yourself grow.

The real question is, do you have the resiliency and perseverance to show up every day to put in the work to make it happen? It's up to you, not me.

# 1% Impact:
## One Thing You Can Do Today to Increase Collaboration

Ask someone for their input or feedback.

- Reach out to a colleague, friend, or team member and ask for their perspective or suggestions on a project, idea, or decision you're working on.

Examples: "What do you think about this approach?" "I'd love to hear your ideas on improving this process."

"Could you review this draft and share your thoughts?"

*Check it off your list and celebrate the WIN!*

**Why it Matters:** Inviting input shows respect for others' ideas and fosters a sense of teamwork. It opens the door for better communication, mutual problem-solving, and a stronger collaborative relationship.

## BONUS TRAINING:
## How to Increase Collaboration Using Discipline

I've created a free training for you to start integrating discipline into roles, communication, and accountability. This will allow you to create a collaborative team environment that operates with precision and purpose in work, life, and community. You can watch it free at:

erikwestrumbook.com/training, or scan the QR code

# The 1% Impact – Transform Your Life Worksheet

When do you feel like you have the most stability in your life?

_____
_____
_____
_____
_____

What keeps you from being consistent when implementing something new in your life?

_____
_____
_____
_____
_____

Do you perform better when working with or competing against others?

_____
_____
_____
_____
_____

# WHAT

The journey of life.

The impact 1% has on you.

The inspiration you will find in life.

The internal desire to always show up.

# Resiliency vs. Perseverance

As I lay on my back on a makeshift training table in the back of an ice arena in Fribourg, Switzerland, I realized the entire hockey game was a blur. I could only remember the last moments of it: I had been blindsided at center ice with an elbow to the back of my head. I got up and started crawling toward the bench. My teammates helped me to the bench and soon I was on the ground, vision blurring as I struggled to breathe.

From what I remember, the paramedics brought me into one of the back rooms of the hockey arena. They cut off my jersey and equipment so they could check my vitals. Meanwhile, my wife and son were at home watching the game play out on TV, not knowing what had happened or if I was okay.

They were in the dark.

So was I.

I don't recall what the paramedics said. I just know it was still dark when I was rushed to the hospital.

Three hours later, I was getting out of our general manager's car, wearing a hospital gown and being escorted to my front door. My wife gave me a hug, and I walked straight to my son's room to give him a kiss on the forehead. I collapsed on the bed and drifted off to sleep.

As I write about my experience, I still don't remember the game, the hit, the trip to the hospital, or anything in between. But what I do know is how much the numerous hits have taken a toll on my life. To this day I am impacted by the effects of post-concussion syndrome, which vary depending on the day.

Since retiring from hockey and concussions both, I've managed to go back to school for my MBA, run successful businesses, author a book (and now a second), and speak around the world. It's only been possible because of the resiliency and perseverance that I learned through playing hockey. But what is the difference between the two, and how do you utilize each in its own way?

Resilience and perseverance are two sides of the same coin when it comes to overcoming challenges. Both are crucial for navigating life's inevitable setbacks, but they emphasize various aspects of the process.

### Resilience

- **Bouncing Back:** The ability to recover quickly from difficulties and adapt to change. Not easy, but required in life. Keep going.

- **Focus:** Resilience emphasizes emotional strength and the ability to maintain a positive outlook even in the face of adversity. The power of the mind at its best.

- **Example:** Someone who loses their job but maintains a positive attitude and actively seeks new opportunities demonstrates resilience.

## Perseverance

- **Steadfast Effort:** The determination to continue working towards a goal despite obstacles or setbacks. You control the outcome with hard work.

- **Focus:** Perseverance emphasizes the action and continued effort required to overcome challenges.

- **Example:** A student who keeps studying despite finding a subject difficult demonstrates perseverance.

The constructive collaboration between the two is evident as you look into both resilience and perseverance to see how they are needed for true success.

- Resilience helps you weather the storms that inevitably arise while pursuing your goals.

- Perseverance keeps you moving forward even when the going gets tough.

## Think of it like this:

- Imagine resilience as the shock absorber in your car, smoothing out the bumps on the road.

- Perseverance is the engine that keeps you driving forward, no matter the obstacles. This reminds me of the book I read as a kid, *The Little Engine That Could*.

Here are some tips for developing both resilience and perseverance:

- **Resilience:** Practice positive self-talk, focus on what you can control, and build a dedicated support system.

- **Perseverance:** Once again, set SMART goals (Specific, Measurable, Achievable, Relevant, and Timely), break down large tasks into smaller steps, and reward yourself for progress.

Challenges are a normal part of life. By cultivating both resilience and perseverance, you'll be better equipped to navigate them and achieve your goals.

## The Overlap

- Both resilience and perseverance are crucial for overcoming adversity and achieving success.

- They often work together: resilience helps you bounce back from setbacks encountered while persistently pursuing your goals.

## Key Differences

- **Focus:** Resilience emphasizes recovering from challenges, while perseverance emphasizes pushing through them.

- **Process vs. Outcome:** Resilience is more about the process of navigating difficulty, while perseverance is more about achieving a specific outcome.

## When to Use Each Term

- **Use "resilience"** when referring to the ability to bounce back from hardship or adapt to change.

- **Use "perseverance"** when referring to the unwavering determination to achieve a goal despite obstacles.

Resilience and perseverance are complementary strengths. By developing both, you'll be well-equipped to handle life's inevitable challenges and achieve your goals. The ability to bounce back and keep moving forward is essential for success in any endeavor. Success is rarely a straight line, but more of a journey trying to climb to the top of the mountain.

The journey takes extreme discipline, as well as the ability to focus and concentrate on what you want. The 1% can be as simple as looking one step forward instead of focusing on the last step taken. You need to set up a road map with a vision in mind to get to where you want to be in life. Do you have the desire to make it happen? If so, keep reading to get dialed in to make it a reality.

## 1% Impact:
## One Thing You Can Do Today to be More Resilient

Reframe a challenge as an opportunity.

- Identify a problem or setback you're facing and consciously shift your perspective by focusing on what you can learn or how you can grow from it.

Examples: Instead of dwelling on a missed deadline, focus on improving time management. After a tough conversation, reflect on how you can enhance your communication skills.

***Check it off your list and celebrate the WIN!***

**Why it Matters:** Resilience and perseverance grow when you respond to adversity with a proactive and positive mindset. Reframing challenges helps you see obstacles as opportunities, building mental strength and adaptability.

# FREE TRAINING:
## Three Keys to Building Resilience and Perseverance TODAY

By embracing a growth mindset, mastering emotional regulation, and leveraging a strong support system, you can become more resilient and persevere through life's challenges. I've created a free training for you to start by utilizing three simple keys to unlock your potential. You can watch it free at: erikwestrumbook.com/training, or scan the QR code

## Focus vs. Concentration

Yogi Berra once said, "Ninety percent of the game is half mental." When you reread the quote, it obviously doesn't make sense, but what I think Yogi was trying to say is that the mental game is key. Unfortunately, it's one of the last athletic tools to be unlocked, and at the elite level, probably the most important. I work with everyone from CEOs to elite athletes, and they all face the same obstacle: their minds. They struggle to overcome mental barriers they've created.

By understanding the distinction between focus and concentration and applying these tips, you can harness your attention more effectively and achieve greater productivity in your endeavors. The terms *focus* and *concentration* are often used interchangeably, but there's a subtle difference between them.

### Focus

- **Directing Attention:** Focus is the act of directing your attention towards a specific task, object, or goal. It's like choosing a channel on a TV.

- **Broader Scope:** Focus can encompass a wider range of things. You can focus on a cluttered desk to decide what to tackle first or focus on a particular area in a busy room to have a conversation.

- **Shorter Duration:** Focus can be maintained for shorter periods, especially when faced with distractions.

## Concentration

- **Sustained Attention:** Concentration is the ability to maintain that focus for an extended period. It's like locking into that chosen channel and truly absorbing the content.

- **Narrow Scope:** Concentration narrows your attention to exclude distractions. You block out surrounding noise or competing thoughts to fully engage with the task at hand.

- **Longer Duration:** Concentration allows for deeper processing of information and better performance on a specific task.

## Analogy: Flashlight vs. Spotlight

- Think of **focus** as a flashlight. You can aim it in a general direction to illuminate a broad area.

- **Concentration** is like a spotlight. You take that focused beam and concentrate it on a specific point for a more intense and detailed view.

## The Relationship Between Focus and Concentration

Focus is a prerequisite for concentration. You can't concentrate on something unless you first focus your attention on it. However, it's possible to focus on something without achieving deep concentration. This can be seen when you have a plan and set goals for your destination rather than just going about things aimlessly.

Imagine what it would be like if you boarded an airplane and the pilot announced, "Welcome aboard, and thank you for flying with us today. Our final destination is Hawaii, but we are not sure if we will make it or not. We are going to try flying without air traffic control input. This is the first time we've attempted this feat, but we do have a combined 10,000 hours of experience and are sure we can pull it off."

Hmm…sounds fishy to me! Would *you* trust them to get you to your destination without using the flight plan, the input from the control tower, or the technology in the cockpit? I'm fairly sure we'd all volunteer to give up our seat and hop on the next flight instead.

On a more serious note, this is how most people go about their days, months, years, and even their entire lives. Without a plan, you don't have a chance to level up your life and change. But even with a plan, you still need to have the focus and concentration to execute. For example, you might focus on your messy desk, overwhelmed by the clutter, but various thoughts and distractions might prevent you from truly concentrating on what needs to be tackled first. It's the same thing when a pilot takes off. Even with the correct flight plan, communication, and technology, the pilot needs to maintain focus and concentration on the step-by-step process.

This is also true for you as you look to level up your life every day. Here are some tips and tricks to consider when faced with a decision to stay in the same place or move to improve:

### Tips for Improving Focus and Concentration

- **Minimize distractions:** Find a quiet space, silence your notifications, and put away anything that might grab your attention.

- **Set realistic goals:** Start with shorter periods of focused work and gradually increase the duration as you improve your concentration.

- **Take breaks:** Schedule short breaks to prevent mental fatigue. Get up, move around, and come back to your task with renewed focus.

Focus and concentration are two remarkably similar concepts working together to manage your attention effectively. Focus allows you to choose what's important, while concentration helps you delve deeply into it. By understanding these concepts, you can learn to harness your attention for greater productivity and achievement.

I always joke about having attention span problems as a high-performing individual, and I'd venture to say I'm not the only one. With the lack of concentration, you have to be aware of the increased opportunities that come into your life, and the more you need to learn to say no. This was one of the biggest lessons I learned as I continued to have more success in hockey and business. It's okay to say no, because it means you're saying yes to yourself and your priorities that will push you 1% closer to maintaining focus on what you want in your life.

## 1% Impact:
## One Thing You Can Do Today to be More Focused

Eliminate one distraction for a set period of time.

- Choose a common distraction (like checking your phone, email, or social media) and commit to setting it aside for 15 minutes while you work on a priority task.

Example:

1. Identify the distraction (notifications).

2. Create a distraction-free zone (silence your phone, close your tabs).

3. Set a timer and work with full attention on one task.

**Check it off your list and celebrate the WIN!**

***Why it Matters:*** Focus and concentration thrive when you give undivided attention to a single task. Eliminating distractions, even briefly, builds your ability to concentrate and boosts productivity. Over time, this practice can strengthen your overall focus.

## FREE GIFT:
## Discipline Yourself to Eliminate Distractions and INCREASE CONCENTRATION

I've created a free training for you to start disciplining yourself to eliminate distractions, follow structured techniques, and maintain a routine. Get out of your own way. Yes, you can train your mind to concentrate more effectively over time. You can watch it free at:

erikwestrumbook.com/training, or scan the QR code

## Reality vs. Optimism

The most successful seasons of my entire hockey career all have one thing in common: I was overly optimistic. In 2005 when I was leading the entire American Hockey League in scoring, I believed I was the best player on the ice. I didn't second-guess my or my team's ability. I just knew we'd win every game we played. I felt the same way when I led the Swiss Ice Hockey League in scoring a few years later. I was optimistic in every single game, and it showed in the end result.

It was important to look at the reality of my situation, but even more important for the optimism to stand at the forefront. Why? Because studies have shown that the benefits of optimism for athletes include better performance, healthier lifestyle habits, more wins, and less likelihood of burnout. Optimism can fuel motivation and foster a positive mindset, whereas reality keeps you grounded and prepared for any outcome. This is where I fell short at times after a failure, which would lead to my blaming other people and not taking accountability.

Reality and optimism are very closely related when it comes to navigating life. Reality is the foundation—the objective facts and circumstances of a situation. Optimism, on the other hand, is the lens through which we view that reality. Your challenge is to navigate these areas deftly, ensuring that your predictions reflect a blend of hope and pragmatism.

### Reality

- **The Objective World:** Facts, data, and verifiable information about the situation at hand.

- **Challenges and Limitations:** Reality acknowledges the existence of problems, obstacles, and potential setbacks.

- **Importance:** Understanding reality allows us to make informed decisions and avoid being misled by wishful thinking. This doesn't mean you shouldn't dream big.

### Optimism

- **Positive Outlook:** A hopeful and confident belief that things will turn out well.

- **Motivation and Persistence:** Optimism can fuel our motivation to overcome challenges and persevere in the face of difficulty.

- **Creativity and Innovation:** An optimistic mindset can foster creative solutions and a willingness to try new things. This gives you the extra push to try something new and get into a growth mindset.

You have to also look at the potential pitfalls in order to give yourself a chance to truly succeed. I unfortunately didn't avoid the pitfalls my first two years of playing professional hockey. I thought I was better than I was, and I also didn't prepare like a professional athlete. I've found these to be the biggest areas of which to be aware.

## The Potential Pitfalls

- **Ignoring Reality:** Unrealistic optimism, where we deny or downplay challenges, can lead to poor decision-making and disappointment.

- **Lack of Preparation:** If we solely rely on optimism without considering potential roadblocks, we may not be adequately prepared for setbacks.

It is always important to find a happy medium between optimism and reality in order to level up and reach new heights in your life. My best years in hockey were sometimes followed by my worst years. Once you make it to the top, you have a bullseye on your back. Everyone wants to remove you from the pedestal and take your place.

In hindsight, I didn't prepare for these challenges nearly as well as I should have, but I still remained optimistic about them. I should have let a little bit of reality set in to prepare for what the year ahead would bring instead of jumping straight into the next challenge. That is why the ideal approach lies in finding a balance between acknowledging reality and maintaining an optimistic outlook. This is often referred to as *realistic optimism*.

## Benefits of Realistic Optimism

- **Informed Decisions:** Realistic optimists consider both the positive and negative aspects of a situation before making choices.

- **Resilience:** They are better equipped to handle setbacks because they anticipate challenges and have strategies for coping with them.

- **Mental Well-being:** A balanced perspective fosters a sense of control and reduces stress and anxiety.

## Tips for Cultivating Realistic Optimism

- **Acknowledge Reality:** Accept the situation as it is, including both the good and the bad.

- **Focus on What You Can Control:** Direct your energy towards aspects you can influence, rather than dwelling on what's outside your control.

- **Maintain a Positive Attitude:** Believe in your ability to overcome challenges and achieve your goals.

- **Develop Contingency Plans:** While remaining optimistic, plan for potential obstacles to increase your chances of success.

By embracing both reality and optimism, you can develop a more nuanced and effective approach to navigating life's challenges and opportunities. A healthy dose of optimism can fuel your drive and resilience, but it's important to stay grounded in reality to make informed decisions and achieve your goals.

**Examples:**

- **Unrealistic Optimism:** Starting a business without a solid plan and ignoring potential financial difficulties.

- **Reality-Based:** Knowing your business idea faces challenges in a competitive market.

- **Realistic Optimism:** Acknowledging the challenges while creating a plan to address them, remaining hopeful about your chances of success.

Optimism is a powerful tool, but it should be grounded in reality. Optimism is not about ignoring reality; it's about using a positive outlook to navigate through it and work towards a better future. By embracing realistic optimism, you can approach life's challenges with a clear head, a hopeful heart, and the determination to achieve your goals. A hopeful and proactive mindset will ultimately increase your chances of success.

A perfect example of this is when I was competing for a medal at the World Championships for the USA Men's National hockey team in 2004. The year before, in 2003, the USA hockey team placed 13th. That put them in a position where they might not qualify for the Olympics. This meant our team needed to place in the top three and bring home a medal if we wanted a chance to qualify.

Our coach approached the initial meeting knowing we were starting in the bottom four teams, facing an uphill battle to the top. But he told us he had confidence we would come together as a team to compete with the best players in the world. After all, our team had the new, optimistic reality of competing for a medal!

In the semifinals we lost our chance at locking in a silver or gold medal during our match with Sweden. That meant it was time to lay it all on the line in the bronze medal game. We had two options: win and take home the bronze, or lose and go home while being relegated from the Olympics. Our next match was against Slovakia. After three periods the game was tied, which meant we'd be going to a shootout, a series of penalty shots that determines the winner when a game is tied after overtime.

After two shootout attempts per side, it came down to a sudden death shootout. The next goal would win. Slovakia went first and missed. That meant it was our turn. Our coach tapped a young kid from Apple Valley, Minnesota, on the shoulder to take the deciding shootout opportunity for the bronze medal.

That kid was me.

As I skated down the ice, I knew exactly what move I was going to make. I had visualized it over and over in my head for years. I came in close to the net, faked left, then right, and back to my left, where I saw a small opening between the goalpost and the goalie's pad. I released the puck towards the net.

Goal.

Goal!

I had made the winning score, and we won the bronze medal. It was the first medal for Team USA since 1996. Wow, what an experience!

The moral of the story is that when you hit an obstacle or experience a failure, the sooner you can get back into an optimistic mindset, the sooner you can start moving forward. This doesn't mean ignoring the world around you or the impact the past had on you, but it does mean not letting it take the wind out of your sails. You need to step up and acknowledge why you failed or why you stopped short when encountering an obstacle.

Sometimes it's not only about the reality of the situation or if you have an optimistic outlook, but even more so about moving from only putting in the extra 1% when you're motivated to transitioning into a disciplined routine. Do you have it in you? Can you commit to 1% today to improve your current self and pay it forward for your future self? I believe you can.

## 1% Impact:
## One Thing You Can Do Today to be More Optimistic

Perform an act of kindness.

- Do something thoughtful for someone else, whether it's offering a compliment, helping with a task, or simply listening attentively.

Examples: Tell a coworker they did a great job on a project. Help a neighbor or friend with something small. Pay for someone's coffee or lunch. Do something positive for someone.

*Check it off your list and celebrate the WIN!*

**Why it Matters:** Acts of kindness not only uplift others, but also create a ripple effect of positivity. They remind you of the good you can contribute to the world, boosting your own sense of optimism and connection.

# BONUS:
## Who Doesn't Want Their Reality to Be Sunshine and Rainbows? I KNOW I DO.

By anchoring yourself in data and balancing optimism, you can develop the tools to navigate challenges while staying hopeful and grounded. I've created a free training for you to start implementing the balancing act one step at a time. You can watch it free at:

erikwestrumbook.com/training, or scan the QR code

# The 1% Impact – Transform Your Life Worksheet

When and how have you overcome a challenge in your life?

_____

_____

_____

_____

How do you stay focused? What gets you sidetracked?

_____

_____

_____

_____

How would you explain who you are? Is that who you want to be?

_____

_____

_____

_____

# WHERE

Experience it everywhere.

Impact your friends and family.

Inspire others at work and at home.

Choose to show up in your community.

## Motivation vs. Discipline

Every night I go to bed in workout shorts and a t-shirt, with socks in my pocket. Why? So when I wake up, I put two feet on the ground, put my socks on, and I'm ready to go work out. I found that when I started working out after retiring from hockey, I needed that reminder and trigger to get after it in the gym. While playing professional hockey, it was easy to stay active while pursuing a goal and ultimately a job. But once I was done, I would only work out when I wanted to, not when I didn't. And that, my friend, is the difference between motivation and discipline. Motivation is doing it when you feel like it, and discipline is doing it no matter what.

In the end, both motivation and discipline are two powerful forces that drive us toward our goals. They may seem interchangeable at times, but they serve distinct purposes in our pursuit of achievement. Here's a breakdown of each concept:

### Motivation

- **The Spark:** Motivation is the initial burst of inspiration, desire, or need that pushes us to take action.

- **Emotional Drive:** It's fueled by emotions like excitement, hope, or even fear of failure.

- **Can Fluctuate:** Motivation is often fleeting and can be easily swayed by external factors or changing circumstances.

## Discipline

- **The Bridge:** Discipline is the ability to take action and persevere towards a goal, even when motivation wanes.

- **Action-Oriented:** It's about consistency, hard work, and self-control.

- **Sustainable Force:** Discipline allows you to bridge the gap between starting something and seeing it through to completion.

The analogy I like to use is fire and fuel. Imagine motivation as a fire. It provides the initial spark that gets you going. But a fire needs fuel to keep burning. Discipline is the fuel that keeps the fire of motivation burning consistently. That's why I have socks in my pocket—to start the fire in me to get up and get after it.

## Why Both Matter

- **Motivation ignites the flame, and discipline keeps it burning.** Motivation provides the initial drive to start a new project, learn a new skill, or pursue a goal. However, without discipline, that initial spark can easily fade, and progress can stall.

- **Discipline allows you to make progress even when you don't feel motivated.** There will be times when you don't feel like working towards your goals. Discipline allows you to push through those moments and keep making progress, bit by bit.

## Developing Both Motivation and Discipline

It is important to lean into your own self-awareness as you dig into the difficult reality of shifting from motivation to discipline. If it was that easy, then everyone would do it, but it's not. This is why it's imperative to keep yourself accountable daily in order to set yourself up for the best chance at success. Here is how you can get started:

- **Break Down Large Goals:** Feeling overwhelmed can stifle motivation. Break down large goals into smaller, manageable steps that feel more achievable.

- **Reward Yourself:** Celebrate your milestones and accomplishments to reinforce positive behavior and maintain motivation.

- **Develop Routines and Habits:** By incorporating desired actions into your daily routine, they become habitual, requiring less willpower to maintain.

- **Find an Accountability Partner:** Sharing your goals with a friend or mentor can provide support and encouragement, especially on days when motivation dips.

Motivation and discipline are not mutually exclusive; they work together to create a powerful force for achieving your goals. By nurturing both, you'll be well-equipped to overcome challenges, stay on track, and reach your full potential. Then you'll be able to leverage them to achieve your goals. Remember, motivation provides the initial spark, but discipline is the fuel that propels you forward on your journey.

As Jim Rohn, author of *The Keys to Success*, said, "Discipline is the bridge between goals and accomplishments." It's one thing to write down your goals, dreams, and desires, but another to put a process into action to accomplish them. Again, if it was that easy to do—if it was as easy as writing down your goals and they would happen—everyone would do it.

The sad reality is that only a small percentage of people actually write out their goals or construct a vision board. The devastating reality is that of that group who write down their goals, an even smaller percentage of people follow through with action. It is the motivation that gets you going, but discipline keeps you growing.

Working on my own businesses and consulting on many more throughout the years, I have noticed that it's easy to get the motivation to start a company. But in reality, a very minimal number of companies take the next step in creating a process and plan to make it scalable for long-term success. They either get caught up in trying to solve the current issues at hand or swept away in the whirlwind of a rush of immediate success.

Either way, they become consumed with working *in* the business and not *on* the business. Yes, there is a fine line between working "on" it versus "in" it. When you work "on" something, it means you are putting in the work to make yourself and the business better. This is looking from a 10,000-foot view to see what is going well and what can be improved, and then making it happen. Whereas, when you are working "in" the business, you are caught up in the day-to-day operations of work and life. This is the ground-level approach, where you feel like you are just checking items off of a to-do list instead of actually stepping back to see what needs to be changed. It is important to do both in order to make the shift into creating a sustainable and successful company.

The ability to stick to a disciplined physical routine is not easy, with all of the temptation in our world and the desire to take the "easy way." If you can utilize a strategy to keep you accountable to yourself and implement a consistent routine, you will be so glad you did. This will increase your motivation to strive towards becoming elite every day by putting in the extra 1% to get outside your comfort zone and ultimately grow.

## 1% Impact:
## One Thing You Can Do Today to be More Disciplined

Create and stick to a non-negotiable plan for one task.

- Choose one important task and decide when and how you'll complete it today, then follow through no matter what.

Examples: I will work on my report from 3:00 to 4:00 PM with no interruptions. I will go for a 20-minute walk immediately after lunch, no matter how I feel. I will, no excuses.

*Check it off your list and celebrate the WIN!*

**Why it Matters:** Discipline is built through small, consistent actions. Following through on a planned commitment strengthens your ability to stay focused and resist procrastination, making discipline a habit over time.

# FREE GIFT:
## BONUS TRAINING To Your Unleashed Discipline

By setting clear goals, creating consistent routines, and building accountability, you can strengthen your discipline and achieve lasting results. This is one of my favorite free trainings that will help you level up and get dialed in every single day. You can watch it free at:

erikwestrumbook.com/training, or scan the QR code

# Fixed vs. Growth Mindset

Pushing yourself is not easy, but it is doable. You have a choice to get held back by staying in a fixed mindset, or to move your life forward by implementing a growth mindset daily. I learned from my parents and others around me that if I wanted to be elite, reach my potential, and become the best, I needed to shift my mindset from fixed to growth—from documenting my intelligence and talents to developing them.

The shift started in 1993. I was 14 years old, and I had just made the B team for hockey. I was devastated. I should have made the A team. I was better than the other players. I wasn't given the chance or opportunity. It wasn't fair. Or was it? Going through the tryout process, I thought that I just needed to stay within the pack, and I'd be fine. I was set in a fixed mindset. I wasn't okay with where I was, but I relied on being pushed by others instead of using my talents and determination to dictate the outcome by consistently developing as an athlete.

Did I want to be in control or let others control my future? I wish I could say it was an instant shift in my mindset, but it took some time until it clicked. When it did, it was life changing. I went from just blending in, with a fixed mindset, to opening an entirely new door of possibility and potential. The shift was in process.

Entering my sophomore year of high school, I was now in a mindset that I not only wanted to work harder than the best player on my team and the best player on the other team, but the best player in my age group. It was time to put in the work. It was time to move into a new mindset. It was time to grow, develop, and push myself to the next level.

That year I led my team in scoring. I dominated my age level and continued to get better every day, but this was just the beginning of a long road to the NHL. Could the dream of playing in the NHL really happen to a kid from Apple Valley, Minnesota, who had only made the B team in eighth grade? I believed it, and I was going to prove it.

The mind is one of the most powerful tools you possess and the starting point of your trajectory in life. The power of your mind, together with visualization and belief, can create success or failure, happiness or unhappiness, opportunities or obstacles.

This depends on your mindset: are you currently in a fixed or growth mindset? This is a question most people don't want to truly face. They will continue to lie to themselves about where they are in life. Society continues to tell people what they should be doing or who they are, and not what they could be doing or who they can become. Our mindsets significantly influence how we approach challenges, view setbacks, and ultimately, achieve goals. Understanding the fixed mindset and the growth mindset can empower you to develop a more effective approach to learning and growing.

## Fixed Mindset

- **Belief System:** Individuals with a fixed mindset believe their intelligence, talents, and abilities are fixed traits. You either have them or you don't, and effort won't change that.

- **Challenges as Threats:** Challenges are seen as threats to their intelligence, leading to fear of failure and avoidance of difficult tasks.

- **Limited Effort:** They may put in minimal effort or give up easily when faced with obstacles, believing they lack the inherent ability to succeed.

- **Examples:** "I'm just not good at math," "I'm a natural athlete, so I don't need to practice."

## Growth Mindset

- **Belief System:** Individuals with a growth mindset believe their intelligence, talents, and abilities can be developed through effort, learning, and perseverance.

- **Challenges as Opportunities:** Challenges are seen as opportunities to learn and grow. Mistakes are viewed as stepping stones on the path to mastery.

- **Embracing Effort:** They are willing to put in the hard work and dedication required to improve, even if it means facing setbacks.

- **Examples:** "This problem is difficult, but I can learn how to solve it." "With practice, I can become a better musician."

## Benefits of the Growth Mindset

- **Increased Resilience:** Individuals with a growth mindset are more likely to bounce back from setbacks and keep trying.

- **Enhanced Motivation:** The belief that they can improve motivates them to put in the effort required to achieve their goals.

- **Lifelong Learning:** They embrace challenges and see learning as a continuous process.

## Shifting Your Mindset

The good news is that mindsets are not fixed. Here are some ways to cultivate a growth mindset:

- **Focus on Effort:** Recognize and praise the effort you put in, not just the outcome.

- **Embrace Challenges:** See challenges as opportunities to learn and grow.

- **Learn from Mistakes:** View mistakes as valuable learning experiences.

- **Celebrate Progress:** Acknowledge your progress, no matter how small.

**Seek Inspiration:** Read stories of successful people who overcame challenges.

By understanding the differences between a fixed and a growth mindset, you can take charge of your own learning and development. By adopting a growth mindset, you'll be better equipped to embrace challenges, persevere through difficulties, and ultimately achieve your full potential. Remember, mindsets are not fixed. It's up to you where you put your time and energy to make a 1% impact in your life. But it starts with taking one step forward into the unknown. Are you ready?

## 1% Impact: One Thing You Can Do Today to Create a Growth Mindset

Embrace a challenge or learn something new.

- Choose one activity today that pushes you slightly out of your comfort zone or teaches you a new skill, and approach it with curiosity and a willingness to grow.

Examples: Try to solve a problem you've been avoiding, and view mistakes as learning opportunities. Read an article on a topic you've always been curious about.

*Check it off your list and celebrate the WIN!*

***Why it Matters:*** A growth mindset thrives on effort, learning, and embracing challenges. Actively seeking opportunities to stretch yourself builds the belief that you can improve through dedication and persistence.

## BONUS TRAINING:
## Moving Into a Growth Mindset NOW

By embracing challenges, valuing feedback, and reflecting on growth, you can consistently cultivate and stay in a growth mindset. This will enable and empower you to develop and maintain a growth mindset while striving to become a new you. You can watch this training for free at: erikwestrumbook.com/training, or scan the QR code

# Time vs. Priority Management

In my book *Becoming Elite*, I talk about managing white space and how it can affect your time management and what you prioritize in life. These small moments of "white space" —when we have time to pause and reflect, go for a walk, or just breathe deeply for a few moments—are what give balance and flow and comprehension to our lives as a larger whole. This applies to how you create the 1% impact in your life on a consistent basis, but with intention.

The ability to complete the task at hand is what you learn at an early age. Make your bed: check. Clean the playroom: check. Do your homework: check. Now what? Without direction in our lives and being told what we "should" do, we miss the point of what we are born to do. How we use our time is vital to how we impact ourselves and others in the world.

Yes, it is important to make a list of what you want to accomplish today and tomorrow. Yes, it is great to accomplish your to-do list. The majority of people stop there. They "accomplish" what they are told to do by their parents, their teachers, their coaches, their bosses, their communities, their friends, and their families. We usually don't have time to reflect on what went well versus what could have been better.

This is where the ability to manage white space comes into play. It can help you take control of your life, your career, your family, and your future. The need for white space is what helps keep you in a growth versus fixed mindset and gives you the ability to focus on today. It allows you to stop and prioritize your life 1% at a time.

Both time management and priority management are crucial for staying organized and productive. They address various aspects of how you handle your tasks. Here's a breakdown of each concept and how they work together:

## Time Management

- **Focus:** Effective use of your time.

- **Strategies:** Techniques like time blocking, scheduling, and creating to-do lists help you allocate specific time slots for different activities.

- **Benefits:** Reduces procrastination, increases productivity, and minimizes overwhelmed feelings.

**Analogy:** Think of time management as filling a container. You have a limited amount of time (the container), and you want to fit in as many important tasks (the objects) as possible.

## Priority Management

- **Focus:** Deciding which tasks are most important.

- **Strategies:** Techniques like the ABC method help you categorize tasks based on urgency and importance.

    A – High Priority, B – Medium Priority, C – Low Priority

- **Benefits:** Ensures you focus on the most impactful tasks first, reduces wasted time on trivial activities, and helps you achieve your goals more effectively.

**Analogy:** Think of priority management as choosing which objects to put in the container first. Not all tasks are created equal, and prioritizing the most important ones ensures you get the most out of your limited time.

### The Synergy Between Time Management and Priority Management

- **Time management becomes more effective when you prioritize your tasks.** You can then allocate your time slots to the most important activities, ensuring you spend your time on what truly matters.

- **Priority management is more impactful when combined with effective time management.** Once you know what to focus on, you need strategies to ensure those tasks get the dedicated time they deserve.

### Example:

Imagine you have a big work presentation this week. Time management would involve scheduling specific blocks for gathering necessary information, preparing slides, and practicing your delivery. However, priority management would help you decide if finalizing the presentation is more important than answering routine emails.

## Effective Time and Priority Management

- Set SMART goals (Specific, Measurable, Achievable, Relevant, and Time-bound). Again, clear goals provide direction for prioritizing tasks.

- Create a to-do list and categorize tasks based on importance and urgency.

- Schedule time for prioritized tasks, and stick to your schedule as much as possible.

- Review your progress regularly and adjust your priorities or timeframe as needed.

By mastering both time management and priority management, you can become a master of your own productivity. You'll not only get things done, but you'll get the most important things done effectively, leading to greater success in all areas of your life. This will allow you to gain control of your time, achieve your goals more effectively, and experience a greater sense of accomplishment.

After all, we are measured on production in everything we do. In sports, you're only as good as your last game. In business, you're only as good as your last month or quarter. In life, you're only as good as the last time you showed up for someone. In the media, you're only as good as your last post.

If that is true and you are only as good as your last time, then why don't we look at our last time doing something and see what we did well, bottle that up, and see what we could improve, fix it, and move on to better things ahead? This is possible, and I am living proof that anyone can do it. But you need to have the right time management, along with aligning your priorities.

I can tell you that I've failed way more than I've succeeded, but all of those failures are what led to my successes. In sports, I got cut. In business, I got fired. In life, I failed my wife. In parenthood, I was unsure. But I can confidently say that at the end of the day, I used those times of struggle to learn. I let those times of heartache sink in so I would remember where I didn't want to be. I used those mistakes to correct my way. Failure helped me set a structured and disciplined routine, aligning with my priorities and not just checking a box. It helped me reach back into my toolbox of what I needed to change, update, and execute to get closer to making my 1% impact a priority.

What would it take to add one thing per day to improve your lifestyle? It's the trivial things that make the biggest difference. Just think about the compounding factor it will have on your life every year if you change just one small thing each day. If you do one new thing per day for 365 days, that equates to 365 steps in the right direction. That means if you commit to the 1% impact during the next one hundred days, then you'll improve 100% from where you are today. But again, it's your life and your responsibility to take ownership in order to make sure you are accountable for your growth in life.

## 1% Impact:
## One Thing You Can Do Today to have Better Priority Management

Identify and focus on your top priority.

- At the start of your day, list the most important task you need to accomplish, and focus on completing it before anything else.

Steps to Do It:

1. Write it down.

2. Block out time to work on it, without multitasking (focus on it).

3. Complete it before moving on to less critical tasks.

*Check it off your list and celebrate the WIN!*

**Why it Matters:** Focusing on your top priorities ensures you're dedicating time and energy to what truly matters. This helps you avoid distractions and maintain clarity throughout the day, improving overall productivity and priority management.

# FREE GIFT:
## Priority Management Fast Track

If you could fast track your time into creating your priorities, would you? I would. By aligning with your values, categorizing tasks by importance, and using time-blocking strategies, you can develop a mindset that prioritizes what truly matters and fosters productivity. You can watch the free training at: erikwestrumbook.com/training, or scan the QR code

# The 1% Impact – Transform Your Life Worksheet

What motivates you to get out of bed?

_____

_____

_____

_____

How do you stay disciplined in your life?

_____

_____

_____

_____

List your priorities in life and rate them 1 (least important) to 5 (most important). Now look at how much time you spend on each priority. Do these align with each other?

_____

_____

_____

_____

# WHEN

Grind now, shine later.

Start today, not tomorrow.

We all dream, but the elite do it.

No time like the present to get after it.

# Responsibility vs. Accountability

Okay, I'll admit it: I have sometimes passed the responsibility for my mistakes onto others. Actually, I could rephrase that and say that at times I've failed to take accountability, but instead blamed others for my mistakes. Hmm. Now that I think about it, responsibility and accountability are frequently used interchangeably, but there's a subtle distinction between them. Yet we don't always stop to look at the difference, let alone do we want to face the reality of who is responsible or if we should be accountable in certain situations. What I can tell you now is that when I take responsibility and accept accountability in my life, I have success. When I don't, I fail, and I fail hard. Let's examine these terms to understand the difference.

## Responsibility

- **Focus:** Refers to the obligation to complete a task or duty. This is owning it.

- **Ownership:** It's about taking ownership of something, whether it's a specific task, a role, or the potential consequences of your actions.

- **Example:** A teacher has the responsibility to prepare lesson plans, and the students are responsible for completing their homework assignments.

**Accountability**

- **Focus:** Refers to being answerable for the outcome of a task or situation.

- **Answering for Results:** Being held responsible for the success or failure of something and facing the consequences (sometimes positive and other times negative).

- **Example:** The teacher may be accountable for the students' academic performance in their class, and the students are accountable to their teacher for the quality and completion of their homework.

**Key Differences**

- **Imposition vs. Acceptance:** Responsibility can be imposed on someone and sometimes self-imposed, whereas accountability often involves a voluntary acceptance of answerability.

- **Focus:** Responsibility is about the task itself, while accountability emphasizes the outcome.

- **Perspective:** Responsibility is internal, focusing on your ownership of a task. Accountability is external, focusing on being answerable to someone or something else.

- **Singularity vs. Duality:** Responsibility can be individual, while accountability can be shared among multiple people.

- **Delegation:** Responsibility for a task can be delegated, but accountability for the outcome usually cannot be fully delegated.

## The Relationship Between Responsibility and Accountability

These concepts are often intertwined, which makes it hard for us as individuals to delineate the difference. It's about focusing on what we control versus how others impact the outcome. A quote I love about responsibility is "It is easy to dodge our responsibilities, but we cannot dodge the consequences of dodging our responsibilities." Just think that this quote came from Josiah Stamp in the early 1900s.

In a similar line of thinking, I've always been drawn to this quote by the 1700s author Thomas Paine: "A body of men holding themselves accountable to nobody ought not to be trusted by anybody." As we look at the two quotes side by side, you can see how closely they are related and how they go hand in hand. But the question is, can you strive to make a 1% difference in approaching responsibility and accountability in your own life?

- **Responsibility is a prerequisite for accountability.** You can't be accountable for something you're not responsible for. This is the foundation you are setting.

- **Accountability strengthens the sense of responsibility.** Knowing you'll be held answerable for the outcome can motivate you to fulfill your responsibilities more effectively.

## Examples:

- **Doctors** are responsible for diagnosing and treating patients (responsibility). They are also accountable to their patients, medical board, and licensing body for the quality of care they provide (accountability).

- **Team leaders** are responsible for delegating tasks to team members (responsibility). They are accountable for the overall success of the project and the performance of their team (accountability).

### The Power of Both and Why

- **A powerful sense of responsibility** ensures tasks are completed diligently.

- **Effective accountability** provides a framework for measuring success and identifying areas for improvement.

By understanding and embracing both responsibility and accountability, you can contribute more effectively in any situation, be it at work, in relationships, or in your personal endeavors. Just think of the power it will have on you and those you impact each day. Wow!

### The Power of Positive Accountability

- **Increased Ownership:** When held accountable in a positive way, individuals are more likely to take ownership of their tasks and strive for excellence.

- **Improved Performance:** Clear expectations and accountability can lead to better results and higher quality work.

- **Stronger Relationships:** Open communication and mutual accountability can foster trust and collaboration within teams.

### Tips for Fostering Positive Accountability

- **Set SMART goals** (Specific, Measurable, Achievable, Relevant, and Time-bound). Sound familiar? Yep, it's all about goal setting and visualizing the end result while focusing on the 1% impact you can make each day.

- **Communicate expectations clearly.** I grew up with my dad telling me not to ASSUME anything, because that will just make an ASS out of U and ME.

- **Provide regular feedback and support.** Repeat what I just said: communicate, communicate, communicate. It's true about feedback—be honest and don't hold back.

- **Celebrate successes and acknowledge achievements.** This is what I teach in the Becoming Elite program. Pat yourself on the back every now and again—you deserve it.

- **Create a culture of open communication and shared responsibility.** Community is so important, and with that comes trust.

By understanding the nuances of responsibility and accountability, you can take ownership of your tasks, deliver better results, and build stronger relationships in both personal and professional settings. I can still remember my first training camp and how I blamed others for my not making the NHL roster, but in hindsight I wasn't ready, and I didn't deserve it. I didn't take ownership, and I sidestepped the reasons I failed. Yes, I was drafted, signed a contract, and made it to training camp, but that didn't mean I was guaranteed anything next.

In my third year of playing professional hockey, when I finally took responsibility for my actions and addressed the lack of accountability I continued to have year after year, I thrived and succeeded at the highest level. I finally had the courage to look myself in the mirror and put the fear of failure behind me in order to step up 1% at a time to get to the NHL.

This was a dream come true, but it wasn't easy. If everything was easy in life, then we'd all do it. What I do know is if you've come this far in the book, you do have courage, and that is what's up next: fear vs courage. Step up and take ownership of your past to create the future you want.

## 1% Impact:
## One Thing You Can Do Today
## to be More Accountable

Share your goals with someone and set a check-in.

- Tell a trusted friend, colleague, or mentor about a specific goal you want to achieve today and agree on a time to check in with them later to report your progress.

Steps to Do It:

1. Write down the goal you want to complete today.

2. Tell someone about it and set a time to follow up.

3. When you check-in, be honest about what happened (good and bad).

***Check it off your list and celebrate the WIN!***

**Why it Matters:** Accountability grows when you make your goals known to others. Knowing that someone will check on your progress helps reinforce your commitment and increases the likelihood of following through.

## FREE GIFT:
## BONUS TRAINING To Level Up Your Accountability
## FOR REAL THIS TIME

Nothing new on how to make sure you don't keep throwing out empty promises. Be ACCOUNTABLE. HOW? Clarify your goals, track your progress, and create a support system. Then you can elevate your accountability and consistently achieve what you set out to accomplish. Watch the training for free at: erikwestrumbook.com/training, or scan the QR code

# Fear vs. Courage

Nelson Mandela once said, "Courage is not the absence of fear, but the triumph over it. The brave man is not he who does not feel afraid, but he who conquers that fear." When you think about it, fear without action goes nowhere. But fear plus action equals courage.

Again, think about that for a minute. If you allow your fear(s) to keep you from moving forward, you won't accomplish your purpose in life. Instead, you will stay put, and sometimes, even worse, take one step back. I also call it paralysis by analysis, because as human beings we get so afraid of the unknown that we analyze it but don't take action. I'm guilty of it on a daily basis, but by focusing on the 1% impact I can make in each area of my life, I can take action and therefore make progress. I'm not telling you it's easy or that I do it every single day, but what I can tell you is that the days you do level up 1% at a time are the days you feel fulfilled and closer to your version of becoming elite.

Fear and courage are two emotions that often coexist. Fear is a natural human response that signals potential danger or threats, while courage is the mental or moral strength to face difficulty or danger. These two emotions often compete for dominance in our minds. While fear can be paralyzing, keeping us safe from danger, courage allows us to push past those fears and pursue our goals.

## Fear

- **Purpose:** A survival mechanism that keeps us safe from harm. It can motivate us to avoid dangerous situations or take precautions.

- **Physiological Response:** This is a natural human response to perceived threats or danger. Fear triggers the fight-or-flight response, releasing hormones that increase heart rate, breathing, and alertness, preparing us to either confront or avoid the threat.

- **Examples:** Fear of heights, fear of public speaking, fear of failure. All of our fears slow us down and cause us to freeze.

- **Negative Impact:** Unchecked fear can become debilitating, holding us back from opportunities and experiences. Think of the anxiety and fear you have. Now address it 1% at a time.

## Courage

- **Action:** The willingness to face fear or difficulty despite feeling afraid. It's not the absence of fear, but the choice to act in spite of it. It involves facing challenges, uncertainties, and risks.

- **Motivation:** Driven by a sense of purpose, duty, or desire to achieve a goal.

- **Examples:** Standing up for what you believe in, taking on a challenging job interview, overcoming a phobia.

- **Positive Impact:** Courage allows us to overcome obstacles, achieve our goals, and live a more fulfilling life.

## The Spectrum of Fear and Courage

Fear and courage are not opposites on the spectrum. We can experience both at the same time. We don't simply switch between being entirely fearless or completely ruled by fear. It's a spectrum with various shades in between. The key is to not let fear paralyze you.

- **Giving in to fear:** This might involve avoiding a situation altogether or letting it prevent you from taking action.

- **Overcoming fear:** This involves acknowledging your fear but choosing to move forward despite it.

- **On one end lies recklessness:** A disregard for danger that can lead to harmful consequences.

- **On the other end lies paralysis:** Being so gripped by fear that you take no action at all.

- **The ideal state lies in courage:** Acknowledging your fear but choosing to move forward despite it.

## Developing Courage

Courage is not something you either have or don't have. It's a muscle that can be strengthened through practice. Here are some tips:

- **Identify your fears:** Understanding what scares you is the first step towards overcoming it. You need to recognize it and address it.

- **Start small:** Don't try to conquer your biggest fear right away. Break down challenges into smaller steps. Divide large goals into smaller, manageable steps that feel less daunting. Take calculated risks to gradually build your confidence.

- **Seek support:** Talk to a friend, family member, therapist, or mentor for encouragement and guidance. Surround yourself with courageous people who can motivate you.

- **Celebrate your progress:** Acknowledge your accomplishments, no matter how small, to stay motivated.

## The Importance of Courage

Remember that everyone experiences fear. What matters most is how you choose to respond to it. By understanding fear and cultivating courage, you can navigate life's challenges with greater confidence and resilience. Having courage is essential for personal growth and achievement. It allows you to:

- **Step outside your comfort zone:** This is where growth happens as you transition from a fixed to a growth mindset.

- **Pursue your dreams:** Don't let fear hold you back from what you genuinely want. Take action and remember the equation Fear + Action = Courage.

- **Make a positive impact:** Sometimes the right thing to do can be scary, but courage allows you to stand up for what you believe in. Be yourself and make the jump with your 1% impact today.

Just remember that courage is not the absence of fear. It's the willingness to take action in spite of it. By understanding fear and developing coping mechanisms, you can harness your courage and pursue your goals with greater confidence. I've faced my fears along the way in life, hockey, business, and family. When I sat back, watched, and didn't take action, 100% of the time it didn't work out. On the contrary, when I took action 1% at a time, I had success. Not always instantly, but at some point along the journey. In today's world we want instant gratification without putting in the work, but that's not reality. The question for you to answer is, do you want to be the leader of your life, or continue to follow others down the road of least resistance?

It is good to feel a little fear, but the important part is to transition it towards courage. Courageous people feel fear, but they are able to manage and overcome their fear so that it does not stop them from moving through it.

## 1% Impact:
## One Thing You Can Do Today to be More Courageous

Take one small risk outside your comfort zone.

- Choose something today that makes you a little uncomfortable or requires you to face a fear, even if it's a small step.

Examples: Speak up in a meeting/conversation where you'd normally stay quiet. Try a new activity you've been hesitant about. Have a difficult conversation you've been avoiding.

***Check it off your list and celebrate the WIN!***

***Why it Matters:*** Courage is built through action, especially when we choose to face discomfort. By taking small risks, you train yourself to handle fear and uncertainty, gradually expanding your comfort zone.

# FREE GIFT:
## TRAINING To Add Courage to Your Life and Overcome FEAR

We all have the fear of failure, but not all of us have the courage to get over our fears. By gradually facing your fears, reframing them as opportunities, and taking action despite discomfort, you can reduce their power and grow stronger through the process. Watch my free training at: erikwestrumbook.com/training, or scan the QR code

## Follower vs. Leader

As the great Robert Frost said, "Two roads diverged in a wood, and I—I took the one less traveled by, and that has made all the difference." Are you a leader or a follower?

Being a leader means stepping into uncertainty with conviction, while being a follower often means waiting for direction. The reality is that most people don't fully understand what it means to be a leader or don't have the capability or desire to truly develop the traits to be a leader. Current research shows only ten percent of people are natural-born leaders, twenty percent are born with a trait to become a leader, and eighty-five percent of people are followers. I find this fascinating when I look at the opportunities we now have to become leaders in the world. But first, you have to lead your own life. You have to step up and make a change. You must not follow the wrong people, but instead learn from the right leaders.

It is never comfortable making a change in your life, but if you wanted to stay comfortable, you wouldn't be reading this book. You want to become elite through change. And that change happens by shifting your life from what you are currently doing into something new. It is important to understand that making a shift in your life will require dedication to not being average, but instead being different. A different you. A new you. Not following the crowd, but instead following your plan to accomplish your dreams. Leading your life by committing to the 1% impact you can make each day.

The shift from being a follower to a leader began for me when I first entered the NHL, but I had been growing toward it each year as I worked my way up the ranks in the hockey world from high school to college to professional. The sooner I shifted from follower to leader, the more quickly I had success.

Let's take a minute and go back to my first official NHL training camp with the Phoenix Coyotes. My idol and the best player in the world, Wayne Gretzky, was on my team for our first scrimmage. It was amazing to hear him ask me, "Hey, Westy, do you know who I'll be playing with?"

I responded, "I'll play wing on your line today." Even though that wasn't my position, I wanted to play with Wayne Gretzky. I wanted to follow him like a fan.

As I look back, this was by far my worst training camp ever. I was following someone else, using his way of doing things and not my own way. Was he the best to ever play the game of hockey? Yes. But was I letting others dictate my direction? Yes. And that changed things. Every time he came off the ice between shifts, I came off the ice. I wanted to be just like him, but what action was I taking to do this? Nothing. I was stuck following and not learning, implementing, and growing.

His journey as an NHL player was ending, and mine was about to begin. I wasn't utilizing what I had learned from my previous success to reflect between shifts on what I had done well and what I could continue to do better. Instead, I was enamored by a legend. I was focused on being on the same team as my childhood idol. Yes, it was a story to remember, and I'm thankful for the experience. But I'm even more thankful that I learned from my mistake not to follow others, but to learn and implement as a leader of my life.

This is why it's important to remember it's *your* path and yours alone. The shift you will be dedicated to making in your life should be what *you* need to do, not what others do. What you did yesterday doesn't define you, but what you do today will greatly impact what you become tomorrow. You will need to commit 1% each day to becoming the leader you want to be, not who I think you can be. It's you. You own it.

And because you own it, you need to understand that leaders and followers are two essential roles within a group dynamic that equally affect the success of a team or organization. While they may seem oppositional, they are interdependent.

## Leaders

- **Vision and Direction:** Leaders set an unobstructed vision for the group and provide direction towards achieving common goals. Leaders need to clearly communicate their vision, plans, and expectations.

- **Decision-Making:** Leaders make choices that impact the group and are responsible for the outcomes. Leaders who involve followers in decision-making and encourage participation foster a more engaged and productive team.

- **Motivation and Inspiration:** Leaders motivate and inspire followers to contribute their best efforts and work towards the shared vision. Effective leaders can adjust their approach based on changing circumstances and challenges.

### Types of Leaders:

- **Transformational Leaders:** Inspire followers to achieve their full potential and strive for ambitious goals.

- **Transactional Leaders:** Motivate followers through rewards and punishments, focusing on achieving specific tasks.

- **Servant Leaders:** Prioritize the needs and well-being of their followers and empower them to succeed.

### Followers

- **Support System:** Followers provide a crucial support system for leaders, offering loyalty, trust, and a willingness to carry out the leader's vision.

- **Diverse Perspectives:** Followers bring a variety of perspectives and experiences to the table, which can enrich the decision-making process and increase awareness to help solve problems.

- **Accountability:** Followers hold leaders accountable for their actions and decisions.

## Types of Followers:

- **Enthusiastic Followers:** Actively support the leader and readily contribute to the team's success.

- **Passive Followers:** Comply with the leader's directives but may lack initiative or engagement.

- **Critical Followers:** Question the leader's ideas and hold them accountable, which can foster innovation and improvement.

## The Ideal Relationship

The best leader-follower relationships are built on mutual trust, respect, and open communication. The most effective teams have followers who are empowered to contribute their ideas and leaders who are receptive to feedback, creating a dynamic environment that fosters success. Here are some key aspects of this dynamic:

- **Mutual Respect:** Both leaders and followers respect each other's skills and contributions.

- **Open Communication:** There's a free flow of ideas, concerns, and feedback between leaders and followers.

- **Shared Goals:** Everyone is working towards a common set of objectives.

- **Empowerment:** Leaders empower followers to take ownership of their roles and contribute their best work.

It's important to keep in mind that leadership is not a static position. Followers can develop leadership qualities, and leaders can learn from their followers. Both roles are crucial for the smooth functioning and success of any team or group. This allows the group's members to find their true passion and direction in becoming the best version of themselves each day. The differences in these roles are what makes a successful team and organization thrive.

## Key Differences

- **Focus:** Leaders set the vision, while followers support the leader's vision. Leaders take initiative, while followers generally respond to the leader's direction.

- **Decision-Making:** Leaders make the final decisions, but they may consider input from followers.

- **Responsibility:** Leaders hold ultimate responsibility for the group's success or failure, while followers are responsible for their assigned tasks.

## Effective Leadership and Followership

- **Leaders** who are inspiring, empathetic, and open to feedback can cultivate a strong and engaged following.

- **Followers** who are critical thinkers, adaptable, and take initiative can contribute significantly to the group's success.

**Great leaders are often made, not born.** You have the freedom to choose what you do with your life and how you use your 1% impact to develop your leadership skills. Here are some qualities that contribute to effective leadership:

- **Communication skills:** The ability to clearly articulate ideas and inspire others.

- **Decision-making skills:** The ability to weigh options and make sound choices.

- **Strategic thinking:** The ability to plan for the future and set achievable goals.

- **Delegation skills:** The ability to assign tasks effectively and empower others.

**Great followers** are also crucial for a team's success. Here are some important follower qualities:

- **Trustworthiness:** The ability to be reliable and dependable.

- **Collaboration:** The ability to work effectively with others.

- **Problem-solving skills:** The ability to identify and help solve problems.

- **Initiative:** The ability to take action without needing constant direction.

Strong leadership and followership are complementary forces. By understanding these roles and developing the necessary skills to implement them, individuals can contribute to a more successful and collaborative group dynamic.

Do we need followers? Absolutely!

Effective followers often possess the potential to become leaders themselves. By demonstrating initiative, critical thinking, and a willingness to take on responsibility, followers can pave the way for future leadership opportunities. After all, our world could never survive with everyone being a leader, and that is why both roles are equally important.

Leadership is not a singular position, but rather a quality that can be distributed and shared within a group. Effective teams leverage the strengths of both leaders and followers to achieve success. That is why I'm thankful for all of those I was able to learn from as a follower in order to become the leader I am today. Now it's your turn to do the same thing in your life—to learn from others that have come before you in order to be the leader you strive to be in the future.

## 1% Impact:
## One Thing You Can Do Today to be a Leader

Offer support or guidance to someone else.

- Take a moment to mentor, advise, or assist someone in your personal or professional life. Share your knowledge, listen actively, and offer feedback.

Examples: Help a colleague with a project or task. Offer advice to someone facing a challenge you're familiar with. Recognize someone's strengths and encourage them to build on them.

*Check it off your list and celebrate the WIN!*

**Why it Matters:** Leadership is about influencing and supporting others. By offering guidance or support, you demonstrate the qualities of a leader: empathy, empowerment, and the willingness to help others succeed.

## FREE GIFT:
## BONUS TRAINING On Going ALL IN as a LEADER

You want to be a leader? Then act like it! By leading with vision, building trust, and empowering others, you can create a strong foundation for leadership that inspires and sustains success. You need to watch my free training at erikwestrumbook.com/training, or scan the QR code

# The 1% Impact – Transform Your Life Worksheet

Where in your life are you most accountable? Least accountable?

_____
_____
_____
_____

Where have you used fear to step up to courage?

_____
_____
_____
_____

If someone asked you if you are a leader or a follower, which would it be and why?

_____
_____
_____
_____
_____

# WHY

Improve your life.

Impact and inspire others.

Dream to create a better tomorrow.

Let go of the unknown to control today.

## Thankfulness vs. Gratitude

I grew up learning about being thankful for my family, friends, teachers, and the simple things in life, but I didn't truly understand what it meant to feel it deep inside my heart. Once I was introduced to gratitude, I started to see how the two complemented each other while pushing me to have a deeper understanding of heartfelt appreciation in my life. Without the ability to look at myself and my surroundings with a universal view, I wouldn't truly know what life had to offer.

As I grew in maturity and developed my leadership skills, I realized that thankfulness and gratitude are often used interchangeably, and they do share a core meaning of appreciation. That being said, there are some subtle distinctions between them.

### Thankfulness

- **Reactionary:** Thankfulness often arises as a response to a specific act of kindness, gift, or positive experience.

- **External Focus:** Thankfulness is directed outward, acknowledging something someone else has done for you.

- **Shorter-Term:** Thankfulness tends to be a fleeting emotion tied to a particular event or situation. This is usually the immediate response in the "now."

- **Example:** Thanking a friend for bringing you a cup of coffee when you're feeling tired.

## Gratitude

- **Broader and Deeper Perspective:** Gratitude is a deeper and more enduring feeling of appreciation. It's not just about reacting to positive experiences, but also about recognizing and appreciating the good things in your life, big or small. It's a general thankfulness for the positive aspects of your life.

- **Internal Focus:** Gratitude is appreciation of your own blessings, like your health, skills, or relationships.

- **Long-Term:** Gratitude is a cultivated, enduring state of mind that fosters a more positive outlook on life.

- **Example:** Feeling grateful for your family, your health, or even a beautiful sunset.

Imagine thankfulness as a smile you give someone who holds the door open for you. Gratitude is the general appreciation you have for the small courtesies that make life easier. To go a little deeper on the above analogy, we can imagine thankfulness as a spark—a brief moment of appreciation triggered by a specific event. Gratitude, on the other hand, is like a flame —a more constant state of appreciation that can be nurtured and sustained over time.

Both thankfulness and gratitude have positive effects on your well-being, impacting your life and helping you impact others. You can use the foundation of thankfulness to profoundly move into true gratitude. Just a 1% change at a time can drastically improve the following in your life:

- **Increased Happiness:** Gratitude fosters a more positive outlook on life, leading to greater happiness and contentment.

- **Improved Relationships:** Expressing gratitude strengthens relationships with friends, family, and colleagues.

- **Enhanced Resilience:** Gratitude helps you cope with challenges and setbacks with a more optimistic perspective.

- **Greater Well-being:** Gratitude practices have been linked to better sleep, reduced stress, and stronger overall mental and physical health.

## Ways to Cultivate Gratitude

- **Practice gratitude journaling:** Regularly reflect on the things you're grateful for, big or small.

- **Express gratitude to others:** Verbally thank the people who make a positive difference in your life.

- **Savor positive experiences:** Take time to appreciate and enjoy the good things that happen to you.

- **Practice mindfulness:** Mindfulness exercises can help you become more aware of the positive aspects of your life.

Both thankfulness and gratitude are important aspects of a fulfilling life and a positive and appreciative outlook. Thankfulness is the initial spark of appreciation, while gratitude is the cultivated flame that brings more joy and well-being into your life. By appreciating the good things in your life, both big and small, you can cultivate gratitude, develop a more positive outlook, and experience greater happiness and well-being.

A gratitude jar can be a powerful tool. My daughter created one of these for my wife on her birthday. She wrote positive affirmations about my wife on small sheets of paper, rolled them up, and put them in the jar. She had one for each week of the year to ensure a happy moment to reflect on with gratitude for the little things in life. My daughter knew that this gratitude jar could turn a hard day into one of thankfulness. How simple, but how hard for us as human beings to grasp. Just 1% at a time can make that big of an impact.

As I've grown deeper in my faith, I continue to learn more about gratitude in my everyday life. In Christianity, gratitude is a central part of life and a spiritual practice that aligns with the teachings of Christ. It's the act of acknowledging and being thankful for God's blessings, both big and small, and for who we are as individuals created differently who live by grace. It's also about recognizing God's love and mercy, and seeing God's hand in everything, even in difficult circumstances. This is where the rubber meets the road—being able to forgive others through grace and to realize that it really is an act of gratitude for God's love for us.

## 1% Impact:
## One Thing You Can Do Today to Show Gratitude

Write a thank-you note or message.

- Take a few minutes to write a sincere note or message expressing your gratitude to someone who has had a positive impact on your life (recently or in the past).

Examples: Thank a coworker for their help. Send a message to a friend or family member, appreciating them in your life. Write a quick note to a mentor or support partner.

*Check it off your list and celebrate the WIN!*

**Why it Matters:** Expressing gratitude strengthens relationships and fosters a positive environment. It reminds both you and the recipient of the good in life, creating a ripple effect of appreciation and positivity.

## FREE BONUS TRAINING:
## Be Grateful Today and Every Day

Thank you for reading my book, watching the free trainings, and just being you. Yes, gratitude is an attitude of positivity. You can consistently reflect on your blessings, express gratitude to others, and find meaning in challenges. This will help you develop a deeper sense of gratitude and positivity in your life. Watch my free training at erikwestrumbook.com/training, or scan the QR code

## Forgiveness vs. Grace

Reflecting on forgiveness and grace instantly brings me to my faith. It helps me to find the deeper meaning of who I am and what problems I continue to face in my life, and how to come to peace with today's world. The main purpose of forgiveness and grace is oftentimes not actually in finding an answer or solution, but rather in the continual process of asking questions that leads you to forgiving someone, or in some cases, forgiving yourself. This, in turn, allows you to focus on grace as a means of moving forward and a way to not carry your burdens all alone.

This is the part of the book that urges readers like you to dig a little deeper, ask more questions about themselves, and keep implementing the 1% impact at an entirely new level internally. It isn't always easy to determine where you are in your spiritual journey, but it is a necessity to help you get closer to yourself. Forgiveness and grace are two interconnected concepts that deal with responding to wrongdoing or imperfection. While they're often used together, they have distinct meanings that separate them from the outcome to deal with letting go of negativity and offenses throughout your life.

### Forgiveness

- **Conditional:** Forgiveness is a conscious decision to release resentment, anger, or negativity towards someone who has wronged you.

- **Process:** It can be a complex emotional process that takes time and effort. It is an internal process that allows you to move on from the hurt or offense.

- **Focus:** Forgiveness is primarily focused on the victim or the offended party. It allows them to move on from hurt or anger. Forgiveness is ultimately a choice you make for yourself and your own well-being.

- **Example:** A person who forgives a friend for a betrayal might still feel hurt initially, but they choose to let go of those feelings to maintain the friendship, even though it may take time to fully heal from the experience.

## Grace

- **Unconditional:** Grace is the act of showing kindness, compassion, or favor regardless of what someone has done. Grace can be extended by one person to another, but it's not guaranteed or earned.

- **Gift:** It's a gift freely given, without expecting anything in return. Grace can involve offering forgiveness or a second chance, but it's not always about a specific offense. It's a gift to *you* as well, to free you from the person or offense.

- **Focus:** Grace can be directed towards anyone, even those who haven't necessarily earned it. It can come from a higher power or from another person. It is unconditional love, mercy, or acceptance, often associated with a higher power or a selfless act of understanding.

- **Example:** A parent showing unconditional love to their child even when they've misbehaved demonstrates grace while offering support.

## The Relationship Between Forgiveness and Grace

- **Grace can pave the way for forgiveness:** Experiencing grace from someone, such as understanding or mercy, can make it easier for the offended person to forgive.

- **Forgiveness isn't always necessary for grace:** You can extend grace (kindness or compassion) to someone without necessarily forgiving them for their actions.

- **They are not mutually exclusive:** You can forgive someone and still offer them grace, and vice versa.

## Benefits of Forgiveness and Grace

- **Reduced Stress and Anger:** Letting go of negativity promotes emotional well-being.

- **Improved Relationships:** Forgiveness and grace can strengthen bonds with others.

- **Greater Peace of Mind:** Releasing resentment allows you to move forward with a lighter heart.

Now, let's look at how you can cultivate forgiveness and grace to impact not only your life 1% at a time, but even more importantly, the lives of others.

### Cultivating Forgiveness and Grace

- **Practice self-compassion:** Be kind to yourself as you navigate the process of letting go.

- **Seek understanding:** Try to see things from the other person's perspective.

- **Focus on the future:** Holding onto anger only hurts you overall.

- **Practice gratitude:** Appreciate the positive aspects of your life.

Imagine forgiveness as unlocking a door. The key to forgiveness might be held by the person who was wronged. Grace, on the other hand, is like leaving the door open, even if it hasn't been unlocked yet. It's a gesture of potential forgiveness or acceptance, even if the other party hasn't taken the steps to earn it.

Both forgiveness and grace are important for cultivating healthy relationships and achieving inner peace. Forgiveness allows you to move on from negativity and resentment, promoting emotional and mental well-being. Grace fosters compassion, understanding, and stronger relationships. It can also create a more positive and forgiving environment.

You need to remember that forgiveness and grace are personal choices. There's no right or wrong way to navigate these concepts. The important thing is to find what brings you peace and allows you to move forward in a healthy way. It takes time and effort, but ultimately, forgiveness and grace contribute to a more peaceful and positive outlook on life.

As I started to find myself through Scripture, it was easy for me to fall victim to my past. Letting go of blame was not easy. I didn't want to forgive myself for what I had done to myself, to my wife, to my family, and to my friends. I was not in alignment with what I believed or where I wanted to be. My morals and values weren't being shown through my actions and words. Basically, I was talking the talk, but I was not walking the walk.

That's when I realized that before I could forgive myself and others, I needed to first give myself grace. That could only happen if I relinquished the negative feelings, practiced forgiving others, and saw how those actions and feelings were affecting me. It was time to let go of what was not helpful.

It wasn't easy.

It's still not easy.

I won't tell you that it *ever* gets easy. Just remember that forgiveness is for you and no one else. *You* will be held captive if you fail to forgive—no one else. A therapist and mentor of mine once said, "The inability to forgive is like drinking poison and expecting the other person to die."

We are the ones who suffer by not forgiving others and offering some grace. Once we allow forgiveness into our lives, we allow ourselves to be more at peace. While I was growing up, my mom always said, "To forgive others one more time is to create one more blessing for yourself." It's within us all to forgive others and, of course, to forgive ourselves.

That's why you should know that spirituality is just as important as other aspects of your well-being. By making contemplative practice a part of your everyday life through activities such as meditation, prayer, yoga, or journaling, you will see benefits. Instead of trying to level up instantly with the 1% impact, start with the following one-minute practice each day and see how it affects your life. As you get accustomed to this routine, you can work toward fifteen minutes per day to increase the impact it can have on your life and your goals.

- 1 minute of mediation in the morning when you first wake up

- 1 minute of prayer as you start the day

- 1 minute of a focused yoga pose to regain control of your mind

- 1 minute of writing in a gratitude journal at the end of the night

This will have a powerful effect not just on your ability to welcome forgiveness and grace into your life, but also in finding true happiness in what brings you joy.

## 1% Impact:
## One Thing You Can Do Today to Show Grace

Give someone the benefit of the doubt.

- If someone makes a mistake or behaves in a way that frustrates you, respond with understanding rather than judgment. Show grace instead of reacting negatively.

Examples: If a colleague misses a deadline, offer to help them get back on track. If someone is rude or short with you, pause and consider that they may be having a tough day before reacting.

*Check it off your list and celebrate the WIN!*

**Why it Matters:** Showing grace allows you to respond to others with empathy and patience, even when they fall short. It not only fosters stronger relationships, but also helps you maintain peace and understanding in challenging situations.

## BONUS TRAINING:
## How to Use Grace in Your Life TODAY

It's time to find out how to build a life anchored in grace. This will help enhance your relationships, mindset, and overall well-being. It's time to get out of the dark and into the light. You got this. Check out the training at:

erikwestrumbook.com/training, or scan the QR code

# Happiness vs. Joy

It's no secret that everyone has searched high and low for happiness in their lives. Whether it's from buying a new home, getting that next promotion, buying the newest phone on the market, or even falling in love with the girl of your dreams, you've looked for it. The problem is, these things give you instant gratification, but can leave you feeling empty hours, days, months, or years later.

Why is it that immediately after a team wins a championship, one of the first questions asked is, "Can you do it again?" This doesn't happen only in sports. The expectations in today's world make it almost impossible to find true happiness and joy. Instead, it's perceived to be found in social media with likes, follows, and "friends." This quick dopamine hit to your brain that won't last more than a second or two can only give you a false sense of happiness that isn't truly fulfilling.

Although happiness and joy are both positive emotions, they do have some subtle distinctions. It's important to look deep inside your own emotions to see how you are affected and what makes you truly at peace.

## Happiness

- **Focus:** A general sense of contentment, satisfaction, or well-being.

- **Experience:** Often tied to external factors or positive events. It can be fleeting.

- **Feeling:** Often described as a feeling of calmness, peace, and well-being.

- **Temporary:** Happiness can come and go depending on external circumstances or internal moods.

- **Example:** Feeling happy after receiving a compliment, spending time with loved ones, achieving a goal, or enjoying a beautiful day.

## Joy

- **Focus:** A deeper sense of exhilaration, fulfillment, contentment, and connectedness.

- **Experience:** Often arises from a sense of purpose, meaning, or connection to something larger than oneself. It tends to be more enduring than happiness. Often described as a feeling of intense happiness, excitement, and contentment that radiates outward.

- **Long-lasting:** Joy can linger for a longer period than happiness, even after the initial trigger has passed.

- **Example:** Feeling joy from helping others, creating something meaningful, or experiencing a moment of pure connection with nature or loved ones, or a profound spiritual connection.

Think of happiness as a calm lake. It's a pleasant state of being, but the surface can be ruffled by life's little difficulties. Joy, on the other hand, is like a wave crashing on the shore. It's a more intense and exhilarating experience that can leave an impression. You can also imagine happiness as a gentle breeze, pleasant and refreshing. Joy is like a wave of euphoria, more intense and uplifting.

## The Relationship Between Happiness and Joy

- **Happiness can lead to joy:** Experiencing positive emotions like happiness can create a foundation for experiencing deeper joy.

- **Joy can include happiness:** While joy is a more complex emotion, it often encompasses feelings of happiness as well. This helps spark happiness.

- **They are not mutually exclusive:** You can experience both happiness and joy in your life. Think back to those times in your life when you felt a sense of peace, joy, and happiness. Rinse and repeat. Let's go.

Happiness is often a reaction, a response to something positive that happens in your life. Joy, on the other hand, is a state of being with a deeper sense of contentment and connection that arises from within. You can look at happiness as something that can be pursued as you actively seek out activities or experiences that make you happy. Joy is often cultivated and it can be nurtured through practices like gratitude, mindfulness, and connecting with your values.

You might feel happy (calm and content) spending a relaxing evening at home with an enjoyable book. But you might experience joy (intense happiness and excitement) if you win the lottery and spend that evening reading on a beach in your dream vacation spot. Both happiness and joy contribute to a fulfilling life. By appreciating both of these emotions and finding ways to actively cultivate them in your life, you can increase your overall well-being.

### How to Cultivate Both Happiness and Joy

- **Practice gratitude:** Appreciating the good things in your life, both big and small, can foster both happiness and joy.

- **Savor positive experiences:** Taking time to fully appreciate happy moments can extend their impact and contribute to overall well-being.

- **Live in the present moment:** Focusing on the present moment can help you appreciate the simple joys in life. Savor positive experiences and avoid dwelling on the past or future.

- **Pursue meaningful activities:** Engaging in activities that align with your values and passions can spark joy and fulfillment.

- **Build strong relationships:** Connecting with loved ones is a wellspring of both happiness and joy. This can be done by focusing on positive relationships and nurturing connections with those who bring you joy.

- **Help others:** Acts of kindness can boost your happiness and sense of purpose.

By understanding the differences between happiness and joy, and actively cultivating both of them in your life, you can experience a greater sense of well-being and fulfillment. As a Christian, it brings me back to the biblical teachings about happiness being merely external, fleeting, and only achievable on earth. Yes, happiness is important, but not the end of our search for more. Joy, on the other hand, is internal, selfless, sacrificial, and a spiritual connection with God.

Whether you are a believer or not, understand that *you* are in control of your mind and what you focus on in life. What are you going to do with your 1% each day, week, month, and year?

# 1% Impact:
# One Thing You Can Do Today to Add More Joy

Do something fun or creative for yourself.

- Take a break today to do something that brings you joy, whether it's a hobby, a favorite activity, or simply something playful that lifts your spirits.

Examples: Listen to your favorite music. Take a walk in nature. Draw, write, or engage in a creative activity you love. Treat yourself to something small, like a snack or time to relax.

*Check it off your list and celebrate the WIN!*

**Why it Matters:** Adding moments of joy throughout your day helps reduce stress and boosts your mood. It reminds you to enjoy the present moment and fosters a sense of well-being, making the day more fulfilling and energizing.

## FREE GIFT:
## BONUS TRAINING to Find Your True Happiness and Joy in Life

Don't Worry. Be Happy. Easy to say, but hard to do. How do you find true happiness? What does it mean and how does it feel to find joy in your life? Check out the bonus training I created for you at:

erikwestrumbook.com/training, or scan the QR code

# The 1% Impact – Transform Your Life Worksheet

What are you most thankful for in your life?

_____
_____
_____
_____
_____

Who do you need to forgive in your life?

_____
_____
_____
_____
_____

What makes you genuinely happy in life?

_____
_____
_____
_____
_____

# HOW

Just do it.

Implement it now.

Get out of your own way.

Go all in on what you want today.

## Outcome vs. Process

I have noticed that people who focus on the outcome of what they want to accomplish instead of digging into the process to get them there are often sidetracked from the path to achieving true success. In my first years of professional hockey, I concentrated so much on making it to the NHL that I forgot what the process and plan to get to the top even looked like. I had to reset and recalibrate where I was vs. where I wanted to be. I was focusing on the outcome and the destination instead of what got me there in the first place, the love of the process.

In year one, when I didn't make the final NHL roster, I was sent to the minor league team in Springfield, Massachusetts. I didn't want to face the reality of the situation and wanted to find an easy way out, but instead this only got me a two-year stint with the minor league team. I instantly started blaming other people and didn't take ownership of what I controlled.

Fast forward to year three. I was sent to the minors again, but this time I focused on the 1% impact I could make each day. I played for Team USA in November of that year, got called up to the NHL in February, and scored the game-winning goal for Team USA to win a bronze medal in May. This was one of the first times I learned to separate myself from the outcome and focus on the process. Understanding the difference between outcome and process can help you achieve better results and foster a more mindful approach to your goals.

## Outcome

- **Focus:** The end result or final product of your efforts and course of action.

- **Examples:**

  - The final grade you receive on an exam (educational outcome).

  - The profit earned by a business (financial outcome).

  - The feeling of accomplishment after completing a challenging task (personal outcome).

  - Winning a competition (team outcome).

- **External Focus:** Outcomes are often influenced by external factors that may or may not be entirely within your control.

- **Importance:** Outcomes tell you whether you achieved your goals or objectives.

- **Measurement:** Outcomes can be qualitative (descriptive) or quantitative (numerical).

## Process

- **Focus:** The journey or series of steps you take to achieve an outcome.

- **Examples:**
  - Studying for weeks leading up to an exam.
  - Developing a marketing strategy to launch a product.
  - Breaking down a large project into manageable tasks.
  - Practicing for a competition.
- **Internal Focus:** The process is within your control. You can influence it by putting in the effort, planning effectively, and adapting as needed.
- **Importance:** The process determines how efficiently and effectively you achieve your desired outcome.
- **Evaluation:** Process evaluation involves assessing whether the steps taken were appropriate and if any adjustments are needed.

Imagine baking a cake and looking at the outcome vs. the process. The outcome is the delicious cake you enjoy at the end. The process is all the steps involved in baking, from gathering ingredients and following the recipe to mixing the batter, baking the cake, and letting it cool. It's important to make the cake before you can enjoy it.

## The Relationship Between Outcome and Process

- **Focus on Outcomes:** Outcomes provide a sense of direction and motivate you to take action. They help you define success for yourself.

- **Focus on Process:** The process is where the real work gets done. By focusing on the process, you can develop the skills and knowledge necessary to achieve your desired outcomes.

- **Outcomes depend on processes:** The quality of your process directly affects the outcome you achieve.

- **Processes can be refined based on outcomes:** By evaluating your outcomes, you can identify areas where you can improve your process for future endeavors.

- **Focus on both:** While achieving a desired outcome is important, focusing solely on the end result can lead to stress and disappointment if things don't go exactly as planned. Focusing on the process allows you to enjoy the journey and learn from your experiences, regardless of the final outcome. A well-defined process increases your chances of success.

For example, you want the outcome of getting a good grade on an upcoming history exam at school. The process would start with attending all the lectures and taking clear notes. You would then review your notes regularly and create a study guide, then practice answering simple questions. Finally, you would make sure you got a good night's sleep before the exam.

Now let's look at an example from work with a desired outcome of giving a successful presentation. The process would start with researching the topic and creating clear and concise slides. You would then practice your delivery beforehand, followed by gathering feedback and refining your presentation.

## Finding the Balance

The ideal approach lies in finding the balance between focusing on the outcome *and* enjoying the process. Here are some tips from the previous chapters for making a 1% impact in finding balance:

- **Set SMART Goals:** Specific, Measurable, Achievable, Relevant, and Time-bound goals provide clear direction and a sense of accomplishment as you achieve them.

- **Celebrate Milestones:** Acknowledge and reward yourself for completing steps along the way, not just the final outcome.

- **Enjoy the Journey:** Focus on the learning and growth that happen throughout the process, not just the end result.

- **Embrace Challenges:** See setbacks as opportunities to learn and improve your skills.

While achieving a desired outcome is important, the process of getting there is equally valuable. By focusing on both, you can gain a sense of accomplishment, develop valuable skills, and create a more fulfilling journey towards your goals. That helps you increase your chances of *reaching* your goals.

As I mentioned when discussing my first years of professional hockey, the benefits of focusing on the process are what lead you to obtaining the desired outcome. Yes, you need to set your goals, vision, and compass on the outcome, but not at the cost of sacrificing the 1% you need to put in each day to reach your version of elite. Here's a look at how I keep that in mind.

## The Top Three Benefits of Focusing on Process:

- **Increased Enjoyment:** Focusing on the process allows you to appreciate the journey and find satisfaction in the effort you put in. I wasn't enjoying the journey in the beginning because I was so focused on the end result. As I recalibrated and enjoyed the process, I had more success and more enjoyment as a person and player.

- **Improved Learning:** The process provides opportunities to learn from mistakes and refine your skills. When you separate from the outcome, you have the ability to not let your failures define you. Instead, you use your shortcomings to learn, grow, adapt, and try again without fear of failure.

- **Greater Resilience:** When you focus on the process, setbacks become learning experiences rather than failures, making you more resilient in the face of challenges. Along with improved learning, this is what defines the elite: perseverance, hard work, not giving up, moving forward from the past, and shifting into an entirely new gear that you never knew existed.

While achieving a positive outcome is desirable, focusing on the process allows you to develop valuable skills, gain knowledge, and build resilience—all of which contribute to your overall success. Putting in an extra 1% creates the new you, the one who has pushed the barrier and overcome the challenges of the past.

Remember, you are in control of what you put in at the beginning, and that means you're in control of what you want to get at the end. Outcome goals are a result you hope to achieve, while process goals are steps and methods you will need to repeat to achieve that result. Now it's time to put a plan together and strategize on what comes next.

## 1% Impact:
## One Thing You Can Do Today to Create a Process

Map out a step-by-step plan for a task.

- Choose one recurring task or project today and break it down into a clear, actionable process. Write out each step you need to take to complete it efficiently.

Steps to Do It:

1. Identify a task you do often.

2. Break it down into smaller, manageable steps.

3. Create a checklist or workflow that you can follow every time you need to complete the task.

*Check it off your list and celebrate the WIN!*

**Why it Matters:** Creating a process simplifies tasks, reduces decision fatigue, and increases efficiency. Having a structured approach helps you streamline your work and ensures consistent, high-quality results every time.

# BONUS:
## How to Fall in Love with the Process

You want to achieve the outcome, of course. But to achieve success, you need to separate from outcome and instead fall in love with the process. Check out the training at: erikwestrumbook.com/training, or scan the QR code

# Strategy vs. Planning

When I first entered the business world, it was as a business owner. I believed strategy and planning just meant I was being prepared, but after a few long months I found out it was far more similar to hockey. You can have a strategy that prepares you for your upcoming opponent, but without the intricacies of a solid plan, you won't have success.

Strategy and planning are two crucial concepts for achieving goals, but they serve different purposes. It's important to understand the differences to see how they will both help you identify where you can make a 1% impact every day in your life, at work, and within your community.

## Strategy

- **Big Picture:** Defines the overall direction and approach to achieve a goal. It's about making high-level choices about what to do and what not to do, considering your resources and the competitive landscape.

- **Key Questions:**
    - What is our desired future state?
    - Who are we competing with?
    - What are our strengths and weaknesses?
    - What unique value proposition will we offer?

- **Competitive Advantage:** A strong strategy identifies how you'll gain an edge over competitors or achieve your goals in a unique way.

- **Adaptability:** Strategies should be flexible and adaptable to changing, unforeseen circumstances.

- **Long-Term:** A good strategy has a long-term perspective, encompassing the bigger picture and considering future possibilities.

- **Example:** A company's strategy might be to become the industry leader in customer service, focusing on exceeding customer expectations.

## Planning

- **Action-Oriented:** Breaks down the strategy into specific steps and outlines the resources needed to achieve them. It's the roadmap that translates the "what" of the strategy into the "how."

- **Key Questions:**

    - What specific tasks need to be completed?

    - Who is responsible for each task?

    - What resources are required?

    - What deadlines need to be met?

- **Detailed and Measurable:** Plans involve setting clear milestones, deadlines, and metrics to measure progress and ensure you're on track.

- **Action-Oriented:** A well-defined plan translates your strategy into concrete actions that can be implemented.

- **Shorter-Term Focus:** Plans typically focus on a shorter time frame, outlining the specific actions needed in the near future.

- **Example:** The company's plan might involve launching a new customer service training program, hiring additional support staff, and implementing new customer feedback mechanisms.

Let's imagine how you would implement both strategy and planning in preparing for a road trip. The strategy would be an overall goal to reach a specific destination (e.g., the beach). This involves considering factors like the fastest route, scenic detours, gas station stops, and potential weather conditions. Your plan would involve mapping out the specific route, identifying rest stops, booking accommodations, and packing necessary supplies. Two similar concepts to help you achieve the outcome, but two different approaches to accomplishing a successful trip.

A lot goes into implementing and executing both the plan and the strategy to ensure the highest level of success possible. The sad thing is, most people put more planning into a trip than they do their own lives. They don't even consider the strategy needed to make sure they set themselves up for success. It often goes unnoticed, but I know you'll make this a priority to implement a plan, 1% at a time, to strategize what you want your future to look like tomorrow.

## The Relationship Between Strategy and Planning

- **Strategy guides planning:** Your strategy sets the direction for your plan, ensuring your actions are aligned with your overall goals. This is your foundation for your plan. It defines the "why" and "what" behind your actions.

- **Planning executes strategy:** Your plan translates the broad strokes of your strategy into concrete steps. These are the actionable steps to help define the "how" and "when" of achieving your goals.

- **Planning brings strategy to life:** A well-defined plan translates the broad strokes of the strategy into actionable steps.

- **Both are iterative:** Strategies may need to adapt based on changing circumstances, and plans may need to be adjusted to reflect those strategic shifts.

In other words, the strategy sets the direction, and the plan outlines the roadmap to get there. Here is another example looking at how a student might approach these concepts:

- **Strategy:** A student's strategy might be to excel in their studies, similar to an overall goal.

- **Plan:** The student's plan could involve creating a daily study schedule, attending all lectures, taking good notes, forming a study group with classmates, and setting aside dedicated time for reviewing course material. This plan is what helps the student accomplish the goal.

In the end, it is especially important to have both a plan and a strategy in order to succeed in implementing the 1% impact to the fullest. Remember, a strong strategy without a plan is the same as having a destination in mind but no roadmap to get there. Meanwhile, having a plan without a strategy is the same as trying to navigate without having a clear idea of where you're going.

This is a common obstacle with entrepreneurs that often prevents them from achieving success. It's not easy to look intently at both and prepare the path forward without getting in your own way. But by combining a well-defined strategy with a detailed and actionable plan, you can increase your chances of success in any endeavor.

As a player, coach, friend, and businessperson, I have always approached life like chess, not checkers. What does that mean? Basically, checkers represents a one-dimensional perspective, while chess signifies a more in-depth, multilayered one. I remember hearing someone say, "Life can be viewed as a chess board, with each piece representing a different aspect of life."

This phrase can serve as a reminder to think creatively, anticipate your next move, and see the big picture. It helps you look at the idea that chess is about strategic accomplishments, rather than fighting over individual pieces. The older you get, the more you'll be able to reflect on how true this is. You might try thinking of chess as looking across the ocean and checkers as looking down a well.

In terms of leadership, this can be applied in the way leaders should look ahead, starting with the end in mind, rather than just reacting to the latest move. I firmly believe that average coaches, managers, and people play checkers, while great managers play chess. Elite people value the unique capabilities of each individual (chess), while average people may treat all the pieces as interchangeable (checkers). I know that I'd prefer to approach life as a chess match to get the full value out of each minute, impact the world, and make the most of my life 1% at a time.

Just remember that strategy defines the game you're playing, while planning details the moves you'll make to win. I can tell you with 100% certainty that if you effectively combine these concepts, you can increase your chances of achieving your goals and vision for the future you.

## 1% Impact:
## One Thing You Can Do Today
## to Level Up Your Planning

Time block your day.

- Take a few minutes to plan your day by assigning specific time blocks for each task or activity, ensuring that you're intentional about how you allocate your time.

Steps to Do It:

1. Review your to-do list or goals for the day.

2. Assign a time frame to each task, including breaks and time for reflection.

3. Stick to the schedule as closely as possible.

*Check it off your list and celebrate the WIN!*

**Why it Matters:** Time blocking helps you focus on one task at a time, reduces multitasking, and ensures that your time is spent on what truly matters. This structured approach boosts productivity and helps you stay aligned with your goals throughout the day.

## FREE BONUS:
## Unlock the Keys to Planning a Path to SUCCESS

You can create a roadmap for success while staying adaptable to life's dynamics. Check out the training to dial in your plan for success through a customized approach for you at: erikwestrumbook.com/training, or scan the QR code

# Goals vs. Vision

As a young boy I dreamed of playing professional hockey, but I didn't realize what it would take to make it to the top. My goal was to play in the NHL, and my vision was to play against the best players in the world. Did I believe that I could become the 1% and play in the NHL, or did I question myself? I'm not going to lie and say I never second-guessed myself, but what I am going to tell you is that every time I set goals with a clear vision, I had a better chance at success.

If you write down and visualize what you want, nothing can hold you back except yourself. You are what gets in the way. Your mind and your lack of commitment to your goals is what holds you back. It's the trials and tribulations that help you develop the characteristics of the most successful people. What type of characteristics have you built within yourself, and how do you tap into your inner self to accomplish what you set your mind to? You need to trust and know that nothing out there can stop you from discovering who you are meant to be.

Goals and visions are both important concepts for planning your future and achieving what you want in life, yet they serve completely different purposes.

## Goals

- **Specific and Measurable:** Goals are specific, measurable steps that you take to achieve your vision. They break down your vision into actionable steps. Goals are clear, concise targets you strive to achieve within a defined time frame. They should be SMART: Specific, Measurable, Achievable, Relevant, and Time-bound.

- **Achievable:** While challenging, goals should be realistic and achievable to maintain motivation. Goals are typically set for shorter or mid-term time frames, providing a road map for your immediate progress.

- **Time-Bound:** Goals have deadlines or target dates to hold you accountable and track your progress. They outline the specific steps you need to take to reach your desired outcome.

- **Example:** "I will graduate top of my class by June 2025 and volunteer at a local environmental organization for 20 hours a month" or "I want to lose 15 pounds in 3 months" or "I will save $5,000 for a down payment on a car in a year."

## Vision

- **Big Picture:** A vision is a broad, overarching statement that describes your desired future state. It's like a painting of your ideal life, encapsulating your long-term aspirations and values.

- **Inspirational:** A vision statement should be inspiring and motivating, something that ignites your passion and gives your life direction. Your vision can serve as a source of inspiration, fueling your motivation and keeping you focused on the bigger picture.

- **Flexible:** Visions can evolve over time as you learn and grow. They provide a guiding principle but are not set in stone. Visions have a longer-term perspective, outlining your ultimate goals and where you see yourself in the future.

- **Example:** "I envision a life where I can use my creativity to make a positive impact on the world" or "I want to live a healthy and fulfilling life" or "I want to own a successful bakery that brings joy to my community."

Think of a *vision* as your destination and *goals* as the milestones or road signs that guide you along the way. Your vision is the ultimate goal you're working towards, while your goals are the smaller, actionable steps you take to get there. Imagine this vision as your dream vacation. Your goals are the specific actions you take to make it happen, like booking flights, planning your itinerary, and making hotel reservations.

- **Vision:** "Explore the historical wonders of Europe."

- **Goals:**

    - Learn basic conversational Italian by March.

    - Research and book flights to Rome by April.

    - Plan a detailed itinerary for a two-week trip across Italy and Greece.

- **Vision:** Become a well-rounded, strong individual.

- **Goals:**
    - Join a gym and work out three times a week.
    - Take a meditation class to improve mental well-being.
    - Enroll in a course to learn a new skill.

## The Relationship Between Vision and Goals

Your vision is the compass that guides you, and your goals are the roadmap that gets you there. Having both a sharp vision and well-defined goals is crucial for success.

- **Vision provides direction:** It keeps you focused on your long-term aspirations and motivates you during challenging times.

- **Goals make your vision achievable:** They break down your dreams into manageable steps, making them feel less overwhelming and more attainable.

- **Vision informs goals:** Your vision helps you set goals that are aligned with your overall desires and aspirations.

- **Goals help achieve your vision:** By achieving your smaller, specific goals, you gradually move closer to your long-term vision.

## Tips for developing both a vision and goals

- **Vision:**

    o Brainstorm and reflect on what truly matters to you and what kind of life you want to live.

    o Consider your values, passions, and aspirations.

    o Craft a concise and inspiring statement that captures your ideal future.

- **Goals:**

    o Set SMART goals (Specific, Measurable, Achievable, Relevant, and Time-bound).

    o Ensure that your goals align with your overall vision.

    o Break down large goals into smaller, more manageable steps.

    o Regularly review and adjust your goals as needed.

By developing an unobstructed vision and setting achievable goals, you can create a roadmap for achieving your dreams and living a fulfilling life. Remember, your vision is your ultimate destination, and your goals are the milestones that guide you along the way. Goals and vision are both important for planning your future, but it's up to you to commit to writing them down to make it real. This allows you to focus on what is important and say no to what is holding you back. Say yes to yourself and implement the 1% impact each and every day to accomplish your goals in order to fulfill your vision.

Your vision can evolve over time as you learn and grow. Regularly revisit and refine your vision to ensure your goals remain aligned with your evolving aspirations. By combining a powerful vision with achievable goals, you can chart a course towards a fulfilling future. Remember, your vision is your north star, and your goals are the steps that guide you on your journey.

Are you ready to succeed? Are you prepared to move forward one step at a time? I believe in you. I believe that you will achieve your goals. I believe you will fulfill your vision. But the question is, do you? If you can say yes, then step up and just do it. Implement it. Execute the plan. Accomplish the goals. Today, not tomorrow.

## 1% Impact:
## One Thing You Can Do Today to Set Your Vision

Create a visual representation of your goals.

- Take a few minutes to create a vision board, mind map, or simple list of your goals, dreams, and aspirations. Include images, words, or symbols that inspire you.

Steps to Do It:

1. Gather images or write down key words that represent your future.

2. Arrange them in a way that is meaningful on paper.

3. Place it somewhere visible as a daily reminder.

*Check it off your list and celebrate the WIN!*

**Why it Matters:** Setting a clear vision helps you stay focused on your goals and acts as a constant source of motivation. Visualizing your desired outcome reinforces your commitment and guides your daily decisions.

# FREE GIFT:
## A Clear Vision Gives You a Clear Direction

What is your vision? Not someone else's vision, but your vision. Create it. By knowing your purpose, visualizing your future, and outlining actionable steps, you can create a compelling vision that guides your decisions and fuels your progress. Check out the training at:

erikwestrumbook.com/training, or scan the QR code

# The 1% Impact – Transform Your Life Worksheet

In what areas do you need to focus more on the process, not on the outcome?

_____
_____
_____
_____
_____

Do you focus more on planning or strategy, and why?

_____
_____
_____
_____
_____

What are your top three goals in life? How do they align with your vision and mission?

_____
_____
_____
_____
_____

# TAKE A STEP

One step at a time.

Take the road less traveled.

Follow your passion and purpose.

You have one life to live, so live it up.

## Two Options

In any given moment we have two options: to step forward into growth or step backward into safety. As you reflect on the importance of the concepts we've discussed in this book, it should challenge you to evaluate your current self and see if this is who you really want to be. Are you going to take the road less traveled or follow the herd? Personally, I believe you are meant for more. The only way you can truly find out is by investing in yourself 1% at a time.

As a hockey player, I was always judged by statistics. How many goals, assists, wins, and losses did I have? The stats were a constant source of stress and contention, but they also helped me monitor my improvement. As a business owner I was measured by profit, revenue, expenses and other less tangible variables. As a sales associate I was measured by contacts, connections, appointments, sales, and revenue.

Do you see the trend here? That's right. No matter what you do in life, you are measured by statistics. One statistic that continues to change is the number of leaders in our world. In a previous chapter we discussed how eighty-five percent of the people in the world are followers, but what do the other fifteen percent do to become leaders?

Here's the answer: they step forward into growth, and they take the road less traveled to create a path for the herd to follow.

You are a leader in your own way, and you have the opportunity to create a vision for your future self. You showed up by reading this book. You made a commitment to finishing the book and downloading the additional resources and tools at www.erikwestrumbook.com. You are the hope in our world, and the time is now to execute and commit to the 1% impact. Not just today, but every day.

Choosing between the road less traveled and following the herd often boils down to personal values, goals, and perspectives.

## The Road Less Traveled

- **Individuality and Authenticity:** Opting for the road less traveled signifies a willingness to carve out a unique path that aligns with personal values and ambitions, rather than conforming to societal norms or expectations.

- **Risk and Reward:** It often involves taking risks and facing challenges that may not be encountered on a more conventional path. However, the potential rewards include personal growth, fulfillment, and the satisfaction of achieving something distinct and meaningful.

- **Innovation and Creativity:** Choosing this path can lead to innovative thinking and creativity, as it requires thinking outside the box and finding unconventional solutions.

- **Self-Discovery:** It provides opportunities for self-discovery and learning as you navigate uncharted territory and learn from both successes and failures.

## Following the Herd

- **Safety and Security:** Following the herd can offer a sense of security and stability, as there is comfort in doing what others have done successfully before. This is okay occasionally, but 99% of the time you follow the herd because you are afraid of change and the challenges that will lie ahead.

- **Social Acceptance:** It often aligns with societal norms and expectations, making it easier to fit in and be accepted by others. This is you getting in your own way.

- **Predictability:** The path is usually well-defined, with clear expectations and outcomes, which can reduce uncertainty and anxiety. Yes, this is all right when you're checking the boxes on the grocery list, but moving outside your comfort zone 1% at a time can make the difference in true success.

- **Collective Wisdom:** There can be benefits in following the herd, such as leveraging collective knowledge and experiences of others to achieve common goals. Follow the right people at the right time in your life to learn from those who have gone before, but make sure they have reached the new heights you are striving for in your life.

How to choose which way to go is the million-dollar question in your quest for what's next. It's important to pause, reflect, and truly look at what you want in your life in order to fully commit to the 1% impact. Here are some things to help you in your journey to decide which way to turn.

## Choosing Between the Paths

- **Self-Assessment:** Consider your own values, strengths, and ambitions. Which path resonates more with who you are and what you want to achieve in life? Take small steps if you are unsure and need time to process what the new you could look like.

- **Risk Tolerance:** Assess your comfort level with uncertainty, risk, and potential failure. Are you more inclined to embrace challenges, or do you prefer a more predictable journey? If it was that easy, then everyone would do it. Yes, you will fail, but get up and try again. Don't stop until you succeed.

- **Long-Term Goals:** Reflect on your long-term aspirations. Which path is more likely to lead you toward your desired outcomes and fulfillment? It's a no-brainer: the road less traveled is your road. This is the road that will lead you to your vision and the future self you've always wanted.

Ultimately, there is no one-size-fits-all answer. In some situations you may decide to go one way or the other, and other circumstances may call for blending elements of both approaches. The important thing is that you're understanding yourself and making the choices that align best with your personal values, ambitions, and vision for a fulfilling life. When you look at your current path and the numerous options that lie ahead, make an effort to choose the road less traveled when you can in search of the new you. You will approach obstacles and challenges on your way, but remember that in order to change, you have to take one step forward to transform your life. And yes, this can be done with just 15 minutes per day.

# The Importance of Change

Change is a fundamental aspect of life, one that plays a crucial role in personal growth, societal progress, and organizational development. You've already learned how to address the importance of change in your life by doing the 1% impact worksheets at the end of each section. Now it's time to look at how change can have a positive impact on your life. Here are nine key reasons why change is an important part of accomplishing more each day:

1. **Adaptation to New Circumstances:** Change allows individuals, organizations, and societies to adapt to new circumstances and challenges. It enables us to respond effectively to evolving environments, whether they are social, economic, technological, or environmental. This is true today now more than ever. With technology at our fingertips, it gets harder to adapt as we rely on others to solve our problems and overcome our challenges.

2. **Innovation and Creativity:** Change fosters innovation by encouraging new ideas, approaches, and solutions. It challenges the status quo and pushes individuals and organizations to think differently and creatively. Always try to think creatively.

3. **Personal Growth:** Embracing change promotes personal growth and development. It pushes individuals out of their comfort zones, encouraging them to learn new skills, gain new experiences, and discover new

strengths. You'll feel the shift as you continue to push yourself from the fixed to growth mindset.

4. **Improvement and Progress:** Change is essential for progress. It drives improvements in processes, products, and services, leading to advancements in various aspects of life, from healthcare and technology to education and infrastructure.

5. **Resilience and Flexibility:** Change builds resilience and flexibility. It equips individuals and organizations with the ability to bounce back from setbacks, adapt to unexpected challenges, and thrive in dynamic environments.

6. **Competitiveness:** In a competitive world, change is often a catalyst for staying ahead of the curve. Organizations that embrace change can seize new opportunities, outpace competitors, and maintain relevance in their industries. You should always be competing with yourself.

7. **Social and Cultural Evolution:** Societal progress and cultural evolution rely on embracing change. It allows for shifts in attitudes, values, and norms, promoting inclusivity, diversity, and equality.

8. **Global Connectivity:** In an interconnected world, change facilitates global connectivity and collaboration. It enables cross-cultural understanding, cooperation, and the exchange of knowledge and ideas. Be open to connecting with cultures around the world. This will

open your mind and heart to endless possibilities in work and in life.

9. **Personal Satisfaction:** Finally, embracing change can lead to personal satisfaction and fulfillment. It opens up new opportunities for achievement, fulfillment of aspirations, and the realization of dreams. Think about joy!

As our world continues to evolve, change is not just inevitable, but necessary for growth, progress, and resilience. Embracing change with a positive mindset can lead to transformative outcomes at personal, organizational, and societal levels. No matter where you are in life, embracing change will help you see how the 1% impact can push you closer to what you want in life, but only if you take action.

## Take Action

It's time to put this all together and take action. Not tomorrow, not next week, not next month, and not next year. *NOW*. Taking action is essential to turning ideas, plans, and intentions into tangible results and outcomes. This is where the rubber meets the road.

Make sure you download the resources and tools at www.erikwestrumbook.com to help you create a plan, stay accountable, and execute. The tools will help you dig deeper into your personal journey to give you direction and meaning in your pursuit of the 1% impact. In the meantime, below are some general tools to help get you started.

- **Set Clear Goals:** Define specific, measurable, achievable, relevant, and time-bound (SMART) goals. Having clarity about what you want to achieve helps guide your actions.

- **Create an Action Plan:** Break down your goals into smaller, manageable tasks or steps. Outline the actions you need to take, the resources required, and any deadlines or milestones.

- **Prioritize:** Determine which tasks or actions are most critical or urgent. Focus your energy and resources on these priorities to maximize your productivity and effectiveness.

- **Commitment and Discipline:** Cultivate a mindset of commitment and discipline. Stay focused on your goals, remind yourself of the reasons behind your actions, and maintain a positive attitude.

- **Take the First Step:** Often, getting started is the hardest part. Take the initiative to begin with the first task or item on your action plan. Momentum builds from taking that initial step.

- **Stay Organized:** Keep track of your progress and stay organized. Use tools such as to-do lists, calendars, project management software, or journals to stay on top of your tasks and deadlines.

- **Adapt and Adjust:** Be flexible and willing to adapt your approach as needed. Sometimes, unexpected challenges or opportunities may arise, requiring adjustments to your action plan.

- **Seek Support:** Don't hesitate to seek support or guidance from others. Whether it's seeking advice from mentors, collaborating with colleagues, or delegating tasks, leveraging support can enhance your effectiveness.

- **Persist and Persevere:** Stay resilient in the face of setbacks or obstacles. Persistence is key to overcoming challenges and achieving long-term success. Learn from setbacks and use them as opportunities for growth.

- **Celebrate Success:** Acknowledge and celebrate your achievements along the way. Recognizing milestones and progress boosts morale and motivates you to continue taking action towards your goals.

It's important to keep in mind that taking action doesn't just involve planning. It also involves executing actions with determination and perseverance. By consistently taking steps towards your goals, you increase your chances of achieving them and making a positive impact in your life and beyond.

In thinking about conversations I have had with the one-percenters of the world, the elite performers, two things come to mind:

First, failing to reach your goals is not always a lack of skill or strategy, but it's usually a lack of focus and discipline. Average people with laser focus become more effective than distracted talent. The 1% impact you can have on your own life will transform you from average to elite.

Second, the ability to work hard and never quit is what sets the elite apart from the average. Hard work is what gets you from your current self to your future self that you envision you want to be.

I've lived my life by these two sayings: "It's what you do when no one's looking that makes the biggest difference" and "If it was that easy, then everyone would do it."

Think about that for a moment. If something was easy, then everyone would "think" they could do it, and we wouldn't have just 1% of people achieving the unachievable. Everyone would be in the 1%. We wouldn't have best-selling authors. We wouldn't have elite, record-breaking athletes. We wouldn't have top-performing employees. We wouldn't have businesses worth billions of dollars.

If it was easy, you wouldn't have to commit to the 1% impact in order to transform your life.

That's why it's important to take action today and step forward in your journey to becoming elite. It only takes 15 minutes a day to improve. Do you want to continue to live your life with the thought of "what if," or do you want to level up your life by committing to excellence 1% at a time to find your true self? I know what you want, but do you believe it? I do.

If you've made it this far in your journey, then it's time to draw a line in the sand, put a stake in the ground, and determine today is the day to stop saying you *want* to change. It's the day you actually *do* it. Be an action taker and do it today. Remember, don't wait until you are "ready" to take action. Instead, take action to be ready.

It's time you step up and commit to the 1% impact. I challenge you...

- to make it a priority in your life. Start by writing down what you are going to do for 15 minutes tomorrow that will begin to make you a better person.

- to find a support system or accountability partner and to go all in on what you want from life.

- to push yourself outside of your comfort zone.

- to make a difference in your life, 1% at a time.

I'll be rooting for you to take the first step towards the new you! Make sure you reach out to me personally to help you make a plan to implement change 1% at a time by emailing me directly at erik@erikwestrum.com.

## The 1% Impact – Transform Your Life Worksheet

What does the road less traveled look like for you?

_____

_____

_____

_____


How will this life transformation change you?

_____

_____

_____

_____


What action steps are you going to take and when?

_____

_____

_____

_____

# Acknowledgements

Writing this book has been a journey of growth, reflection, and immense learning, and it would not have been possible without the support of many incredible people.

First, I want to thank my family for their unwavering love and patience. To my wife, Kelly, your belief in me has been my constant source of strength, and your encouragement keeps me grounded even on the toughest days. To my children, you are my greatest motivation and inspiration. Luke, the light of the world. Ethan, the strength of the world. Isabella, the beauty of the world. Evelina, the life of the world. I love you all to the moon and back.

To my friends, thank you for your endless support and for listening to my ideas, even though they are never-ending. Your feedback and encouragement give me the confidence to keep pushing forward to follow my passion and purpose.

A special thanks to my mom and dad, my mother-in-law and father in-law, and all my family who support every new endeavor I create, chase, and make a reality. Without your faith in me, I wouldn't be able to continue to do what I love.

Lastly, to my readers—whether this is the first book of mine you've picked up, or you've been with me from the beginning —thank you. Your support and encouragement of my work is the reason I write, and I'm endlessly grateful to share this journey with you.

Be Elite 1% at a Time!

With Love and Gratitude,

*Erik*

# Author Bio

Erik Westrum is a former professional hockey player, author, motivational speaker, leadership coach, and entrepreneur at heart. He has had a passion to help others since he was a young child, and this has not changed as he continues to fulfill his purpose in life—to be a Servant Leader.

After playing professional hockey for 12 years, Erik went back to the Carlson School of Management to get his MBA to gain more knowledge and expertise to help leaders and companies grow exponentially. After consulting on numerous projects and coaching hundreds of people over the past 25 years, Erik established the principles and processes through his first book, *Becoming Elite: Transforming Your Life Using Four Proven Pillars of Performance*. As he went around the world to speak, consult, coach, and conduct workshops for people of all walks of life, he always ended with the 1% impact. That is what brought this book to life, and Erik remains committed to leading people to transform their lives 1% at a time.

Erik resides in Prior Lake, Minnesota, with his amazing wife, Kelly, and their four children, Luke, Ethan, Isabella, and Evelina. He continues to guide people, businesses, athletes, and anyone looking to improve his or her life through his speaking, consulting, and coaching. Erik is excited to walk alongside you on your journey to becoming a 1% better you each and every day.

Made in the USA
Monee, IL
01 April 2025